C-1442   CAREER EXAMINATION SERIES

*This is your
PASSBOOK for...*

Public Health Social Work Assistant

*Test Preparation Study Guide
Questions & Answers*

COPYRIGHT NOTICE

This book is SOLELY intended for, is sold ONLY to, and its use is RESTRICTED to individual, bona fide applicants or candidates who qualify by virtue of having seriously filed applications for appropriate license, certificate, professional and/or promotional advancement, higher school matriculation, scholarship, or other legitimate requirements of education and/or governmental authorities.

This book is NOT intended for use, class instruction, tutoring, training, duplication, copying, reprinting, excerption, or adaptation, etc., by:

1) Other publishers
2) Proprietors and/or Instructors of "Coaching" and/or Preparatory Courses
3) Personnel and/or Training Divisions of commercial, industrial, and governmental organizations
4) Schools, colleges, or universities and/or their departments and staffs, including teachers and other personnel
5) Testing Agencies or Bureaus
6) Study groups which seek by the purchase of a single volume to copy and/or duplicate and/or adapt this material for use by the group as a whole without having purchased individual volumes for each of the members of the group
7) Et al.

Such persons would be in violation of appropriate Federal and State statutes.

PROVISION OF LICENSING AGREEMENTS – Recognized educational, commercial, industrial, and governmental institutions and organizations, and others legitimately engaged in educational pursuits, including training, testing, and measurement activities, may address request for a licensing agreement to the copyright owners, who will determine whether, and under what conditions, including fees and charges, the materials in this book may be used them. In other words, a licensing facility exists for the legitimate use of the material in this book on other than an individual basis. However, it is asseverated and affirmed here that the material in this book CANNOT be used without the receipt of the express permission of such a licensing agreement from the Publishers. Inquiries re licensing should be addressed to the company, attention rights and permissions department.

All rights reserved, including the right of reproduction in whole or in part, in any form or by any means, electronic or mechanical, including photocopying, recording, or by any information storage and retrieval system, without permission in writing from the Publisher.

Copyright © 2025 by
National Learning Corporation

212 Michael Drive, Syosset, NY 11791
(516) 921-8888 • www.passbooks.com
E-mail: info@passbooks.com

PASSBOOK® SERIES

THE *PASSBOOK® SERIES* has been created to prepare applicants and candidates for the ultimate academic battlefield – the examination room.

At some time in our lives, each and every one of us may be required to take an examination – for validation, matriculation, admission, qualification, registration, certification, or licensure.

Based on the assumption that every applicant or candidate has met the basic formal educational standards, has taken the required number of courses, and read the necessary texts, the *PASSBOOK® SERIES* furnishes the one special preparation which may assure passing with confidence, instead of failing with insecurity. Examination questions – together with answers – are furnished as the basic vehicle for study so that the mysteries of the examination and its compounding difficulties may be eliminated or diminished by a sure method.

This book is meant to help you pass your examination provided that you qualify and are serious in your objective.

The entire field is reviewed through the huge store of content information which is succinctly presented through a provocative and challenging approach – the question-and-answer method.

A climate of success is established by furnishing the correct answers at the end of each test.

You soon learn to recognize types of questions, forms of questions, and patterns of questioning. You may even begin to anticipate expected outcomes.

You perceive that many questions are repeated or adapted so that you can gain acute insights, which may enable you to score many sure points.

You learn how to confront new questions, or types of questions, and to attack them confidently and work out the correct answers.

You note objectives and emphases, and recognize pitfalls and dangers, so that you may make positive educational adjustments.

Moreover, you are kept fully informed in relation to new concepts, methods, practices, and directions in the field.

You discover that you are actually taking the examination all the time: you are preparing for the examination by "taking" an examination, not by reading extraneous and/or supererogatory textbooks.

In short, this PASSBOOK®, used directedly, should be an important factor in helping you to pass your test.

PUBLIC HEALTH SOCIAL WORK ASSISTANT

In a **Public Health Social Work Assistant** you would serve as a member of a multidisciplinary survey team responsible for evaluating health care facilities to insure their consistency with State and federal regulations. You would participate in surveys, medical reviews and other audit mechanisms to determine the adequacy and suitability of services provided to meet the social and emotional needs and problems of patients. You would consult with the social work directors/administrators of health facilities concerning the quality of existing medical social work programs and assist in the development of new social work services.

1. Health-related casework with older adults
   These questions will be designed to test for knowledge and understanding of social casework principles and practices associated with the long term care of older adults. Question topics may include, but are not necessarily limited to, symptoms of diseases and conditions which affect older adults; treatments commonly associated with these conditions; psycho-social factors related to disease, disability and treatment; the role of the social caseworker and other health professionals in treatment; helping the client/resident access social supports and community resources; working with friends and families of clients/residents; client/resident advocacy; and ethical issues relating to client treatment.

2. Health-related casework
   These questions will be designed to test for knowledge and understanding of social casework principles and practices associated with casework practice in a health-related setting. Question topics may include, but are not necessarily limited to, symptoms of disease and disability; treatments associated with diseases and disabling conditions; psycho-social factors in disease, disability and treatment; the role of the social caseworker and other health professionals in treatment; helping clients access social supports and community resources; working with friends and families of clients; client advocacy; and ethical issues relating to client treatment.

3. Preparing written material
   These questions test how well you can express yourself in writing. Particular emphasis is placed upon two major aspects of written communication: how to express given information clearly and accurately and how to present written material logically and comprehensibly.

4. Interviewing
   These questions are designed to test for the principles and practices employed in obtaining information from individuals through structured conversations. These questions require you to apply the principles, practices and techniques of effective interviewing to hypothetical interviewing situations. Questions are also included which present an interviewing situation in which some problem has arisen and your task, is to choose the most appropriate course of action under the circumstances.

HOW TO TAKE A TEST

I. YOU MUST PASS AN EXAMINATION

A. WHAT EVERY CANDIDATE SHOULD KNOW

Examination applicants often ask us for help in preparing for the written test. What can I study in advance? What kinds of questions will be asked? How will the test be given? How will the papers be graded?

As an applicant for a civil service examination, you may be wondering about some of these things. Our purpose here is to suggest effective methods of advance study and to describe civil service examinations.

Your chances for success on this examination can be increased if you know how to prepare. Those "pre-examination jitters" can be reduced if you know what to expect. You can even experience an adventure in good citizenship if you know why civil service exams are given.

B. WHY ARE CIVIL SERVICE EXAMINATIONS GIVEN?

Civil service examinations are important to you in two ways. As a citizen, you want public jobs filled by employees who know how to do their work. As a job seeker, you want a fair chance to compete for that job on an equal footing with other candidates. The best-known means of accomplishing this two-fold goal is the competitive examination.

Exams are widely publicized throughout the nation. They may be administered for jobs in federal, state, city, municipal, town or village governments or agencies.

Any citizen may apply, with some limitations, such as the age or residence of applicants. Your experience and education may be reviewed to see whether you meet the requirements for the particular examination. When these requirements exist, they are reasonable and applied consistently to all applicants. Thus, a competitive examination may cause you some uneasiness now, but it is your privilege and safeguard.

C. HOW ARE CIVIL SERVICE EXAMS DEVELOPED?

Examinations are carefully written by trained technicians who are specialists in the field known as "psychological measurement," in consultation with recognized authorities in the field of work that the test will cover. These experts recommend the subject matter areas or skills to be tested; only those knowledges or skills important to your success on the job are included. The most reliable books and source materials available are used as references. Together, the experts and technicians judge the difficulty level of the questions.

Test technicians know how to phrase questions so that the problem is clearly stated. Their ethics do not permit "trick" or "catch" questions. Questions may have been tried out on sample groups, or subjected to statistical analysis, to determine their usefulness.

Written tests are often used in combination with performance tests, ratings of training and experience, and oral interviews. All of these measures combine to form the best-known means of finding the right person for the right job.

II. HOW TO PASS THE WRITTEN TEST

A. NATURE OF THE EXAMINATION

To prepare intelligently for civil service examinations, you should know how they differ from school examinations you have taken. In school you were assigned certain definite pages to read or subjects to cover. The examination questions were quite detailed and usually emphasized memory. Civil service exams, on the other hand, try to discover your present ability to perform the duties of a position, plus your potentiality to learn these duties. In other words, a civil service exam attempts to predict how successful you will be. Questions cover such a broad area that they cannot be as minute and detailed as school exam questions.

In the public service similar kinds of work, or positions, are grouped together in one "class." This process is known as *position-classification*. All the positions in a class are paid according to the salary range for that class. One class title covers all of these positions, and they are all tested by the same examination.

B. FOUR BASIC STEPS

1) Study the announcement

How, then, can you know what subjects to study? Our best answer is: "Learn as much as possible about the class of positions for which you've applied." The exam will test the knowledge, skills and abilities needed to do the work.

Your most valuable source of information about the position you want is the official exam announcement. This announcement lists the training and experience qualifications. Check these standards and apply only if you come reasonably close to meeting them.

The brief description of the position in the examination announcement offers some clues to the subjects which will be tested. Think about the job itself. Review the duties in your mind. Can you perform them, or are there some in which you are rusty? Fill in the blank spots in your preparation.

Many jurisdictions preview the written test in the exam announcement by including a section called "Knowledge and Abilities Required," "Scope of the Examination," or some similar heading. Here you will find out specifically what fields will be tested.

2) Review your own background

Once you learn in general what the position is all about, and what you need to know to do the work, ask yourself which subjects you already know fairly well and which need improvement. You may wonder whether to concentrate on improving your strong areas or on building some background in your fields of weakness. When the announcement has specified "some knowledge" or "considerable knowledge," or has used adjectives like "beginning principles of…" or "advanced … methods," you can get a clue as to the number and difficulty of questions to be asked in any given field. More questions, and hence broader coverage, would be included for those subjects which are more important in the work. Now weigh your strengths and weaknesses against the job requirements and prepare accordingly.

3) Determine the level of the position

Another way to tell how intensively you should prepare is to understand the level of the job for which you are applying. Is it the entering level? In other words, is this the position in which beginners in a field of work are hired? Or is it an intermediate or advanced level? Sometimes this is indicated by such words as "Junior" or "Senior" in the class title. Other jurisdictions use Roman numerals to designate the level – Clerk I, Clerk II, for example. The word "Supervisor" sometimes appears in the title. If the level is not indicated by the title, check the description of duties. Will you be working under very close supervision, or will you have responsibility for independent decisions in this work?

4) Choose appropriate study materials

Now that you know the subjects to be examined and the relative amount of each subject to be covered, you can choose suitable study materials. For beginning level jobs, or even advanced ones, if you have a pronounced weakness in some aspect of your training, read a modern, standard textbook in that field. Be sure it is up to date and has general coverage. Such books are normally available at your library, and the librarian will be glad to help you locate one. For entry-level positions, questions of appropriate difficulty are chosen – neither highly advanced questions, nor those too simple. Such questions require careful thought but not advanced training.

If the position for which you are applying is technical or advanced, you will read more advanced, specialized material. If you are already familiar with the basic principles of your field, elementary textbooks would waste your time. Concentrate on advanced textbooks and technical periodicals. Think through the concepts and review difficult problems in your field.

These are all general sources. You can get more ideas on your own initiative, following these leads. For example, training manuals and publications of the government agency which employs workers in your field can be useful, particularly for technical and professional positions. A letter or visit to the government department involved may result in more specific study suggestions, and certainly will provide you with a more definite idea of the exact nature of the position you are seeking.

III. KINDS OF TESTS

Tests are used for purposes other than measuring knowledge and ability to perform specified duties. For some positions, it is equally important to test ability to make adjustments to new situations or to profit from training. In others, basic mental abilities not dependent on information are essential. Questions which test these things may not appear as pertinent to the duties of the position as those which test for knowledge and information. Yet they are often highly important parts of a fair examination. For very general questions, it is almost impossible to help you direct your study efforts. What we can do is to point out some of the more common of these general abilities needed in public service positions and describe some typical questions.

1) General information

Broad, general information has been found useful for predicting job success in some kinds of work. This is tested in a variety of ways, from vocabulary lists to questions about current events. Basic background in some field of work, such as sociology or economics, may be sampled in a group of questions. Often these are principles which have become familiar to most persons through exposure rather than through formal training. It is difficult to advise you how to study for these questions; being alert to the world around you is our best suggestion.

2) Verbal ability

An example of an ability needed in many positions is verbal or language ability. Verbal ability is, in brief, the ability to use and understand words. Vocabulary and grammar tests are typical measures of this ability. Reading comprehension or paragraph interpretation questions are common in many kinds of civil service tests. You are given a paragraph of written material and asked to find its central meaning.

3) Numerical ability

Number skills can be tested by the familiar arithmetic problem, by checking paired lists of numbers to see which are alike and which are different, or by interpreting charts and graphs. In the latter test, a graph may be printed in the test booklet which you are asked to use as the basis for answering questions.

4) Observation

A popular test for law-enforcement positions is the observation test. A picture is shown to you for several minutes, then taken away. Questions about the picture test your ability to observe both details and larger elements.

5) Following directions

In many positions in the public service, the employee must be able to carry out written instructions dependably and accurately. You may be given a chart with several columns, each column listing a variety of information. The questions require you to carry out directions involving the information given in the chart.

6) Skills and aptitudes

Performance tests effectively measure some manual skills and aptitudes. When the skill is one in which you are trained, such as typing or shorthand, you can practice. These tests are often very much like those given in business school or high school courses. For many of the other skills and aptitudes, however, no short-time preparation can be made. Skills and abilities natural to you or that you have developed throughout your lifetime are being tested.

Many of the general questions just described provide all the data needed to answer the questions and ask you to use your reasoning ability to find the answers. Your best preparation for these tests, as well as for tests of facts and ideas, is to be at your physical and mental best. You, no doubt, have your own methods of getting into an exam-taking mood and keeping "in shape." The next section lists some ideas on this subject.

IV. KINDS OF QUESTIONS

Only rarely is the "essay" question, which you answer in narrative form, used in civil service tests. Civil service tests are usually of the short-answer type. Full instructions for answering these questions will be given to you at the examination. But in case this is your first experience with short-answer questions and separate answer sheets, here is what you need to know:

1) Multiple-choice Questions

Most popular of the short-answer questions is the "multiple choice" or "best answer" question. It can be used, for example, to test for factual knowledge, ability to solve problems or judgment in meeting situations found at work.

A multiple-choice question is normally one of three types—
- It can begin with an incomplete statement followed by several possible endings. You are to find the one ending which *best* completes the statement, although some of the others may not be entirely wrong.
- It can also be a complete statement in the form of a question which is answered by choosing one of the statements listed.

- It can be in the form of a problem – again you select the best answer.

Here is an example of a multiple-choice question with a discussion which should give you some clues as to the method for choosing the right answer:

When an employee has a complaint about his assignment, the action which will *best* help him overcome his difficulty is to
   A. discuss his difficulty with his coworkers
   B. take the problem to the head of the organization
   C. take the problem to the person who gave him the assignment
   D. say nothing to anyone about his complaint

In answering this question, you should study each of the choices to find which is best. Consider choice "A" – Certainly an employee may discuss his complaint with fellow employees, but no change or improvement can result, and the complaint remains unresolved. Choice "B" is a poor choice since the head of the organization probably does not know what assignment you have been given, and taking your problem to him is known as "going over the head" of the supervisor. The supervisor, or person who made the assignment, is the person who can clarify it or correct any injustice. Choice "C" is, therefore, correct. To say nothing, as in choice "D," is unwise. Supervisors have and interest in knowing the problems employees are facing, and the employee is seeking a solution to his problem.

2) True/False Questions

The "true/false" or "right/wrong" form of question is sometimes used. Here a complete statement is given. Your job is to decide whether the statement is right or wrong.

SAMPLE: A roaming cell-phone call to a nearby city costs less than a non-roaming call to a distant city.

This statement is wrong, or false, since roaming calls are more expensive.

This is not a complete list of all possible question forms, although most of the others are variations of these common types. You will always get complete directions for answering questions. Be sure you understand *how* to mark your answers – ask questions until you do.

V. RECORDING YOUR ANSWERS

Computer terminals are used more and more today for many different kinds of exams.

For an examination with very few applicants, you may be told to record your answers in the test booklet itself. Separate answer sheets are much more common. If this separate answer sheet is to be scored by machine – and this is often the case – it is highly important that you mark your answers correctly in order to get credit.

An electronic scoring machine is often used in civil service offices because of the speed with which papers can be scored. Machine-scored answer sheets must be marked with a pencil, which will be given to you. This pencil has a high graphite content which responds to the electronic scoring machine. As a matter of fact, stray dots may register as answers, so do not let your pencil rest on the answer sheet while you are pondering the correct answer. Also, if your pencil lead breaks or is otherwise defective, ask for another.

Since the answer sheet will be dropped in a slot in the scoring machine, be careful not to bend the corners or get the paper crumpled.

The answer sheet normally has five vertical columns of numbers, with 30 numbers to a column. These numbers correspond to the question numbers in your test booklet. After each number, going across the page are four or five pairs of dotted lines. These short dotted lines have small letters or numbers above them. The first two pairs may also have a "T" or "F" above the letters. This indicates that the first two pairs only are to be used if the questions are of the true-false type. If the questions are multiple choice, disregard the "T" and "F" and pay attention only to the small letters or numbers.

Answer your questions in the manner of the sample that follows:

32. The largest city in the United States is
    A. Washington, D.C.
    B. New York City
    C. Chicago
    D. Detroit
    E. San Francisco

1) Choose the answer you think is best. (New York City is the largest, so "B" is correct.)
2) Find the row of dotted lines numbered the same as the question you are answering. (Find row number 32)
3) Find the pair of dotted lines corresponding to the answer. (Find the pair of lines under the mark "B.")
4) Make a solid black mark between the dotted lines.

VI. BEFORE THE TEST

Common sense will help you find procedures to follow to get ready for an examination. Too many of us, however, overlook these sensible measures. Indeed, nervousness and fatigue have been found to be the most serious reasons why applicants fail to do their best on civil service tests. Here is a list of reminders:

- Begin your preparation early – Don't wait until the last minute to go scurrying around for books and materials or to find out what the position is all about.
- Prepare continuously – An hour a night for a week is better than an all-night cram session. This has been definitely established. What is more, a night a week for a month will return better dividends than crowding your study into a shorter period of time.
- Locate the place of the exam – You have been sent a notice telling you when and where to report for the examination. If the location is in a different town or otherwise unfamiliar to you, it would be well to inquire the best route and learn something about the building.
- Relax the night before the test – Allow your mind to rest. Do not study at all that night. Plan some mild recreation or diversion; then go to bed early and get a good night's sleep.
- Get up early enough to make a leisurely trip to the place for the test – This way unforeseen events, traffic snarls, unfamiliar buildings, etc. will not upset you.
- Dress comfortably – A written test is not a fashion show. You will be known by number and not by name, so wear something comfortable.

- Leave excess paraphernalia at home – Shopping bags and odd bundles will get in your way. You need bring only the items mentioned in the official notice you received; usually everything you need is provided. Do not bring reference books to the exam. They will only confuse those last minutes and be taken away from you when in the test room.
- Arrive somewhat ahead of time – If because of transportation schedules you must get there very early, bring a newspaper or magazine to take your mind off yourself while waiting.
- Locate the examination room – When you have found the proper room, you will be directed to the seat or part of the room where you will sit. Sometimes you are given a sheet of instructions to read while you are waiting. Do not fill out any forms until you are told to do so; just read them and be prepared.
- Relax and prepare to listen to the instructions
- If you have any physical problem that may keep you from doing your best, be sure to tell the test administrator. If you are sick or in poor health, you really cannot do your best on the exam. You can come back and take the test some other time.

VII. AT THE TEST

The day of the test is here and you have the test booklet in your hand. The temptation to get going is very strong. Caution! There is more to success than knowing the right answers. You must know how to identify your papers and understand variations in the type of short-answer question used in this particular examination. Follow these suggestions for maximum results from your efforts:

1) Cooperate with the monitor

The test administrator has a duty to create a situation in which you can be as much at ease as possible. He will give instructions, tell you when to begin, check to see that you are marking your answer sheet correctly, and so on. He is not there to guard you, although he will see that your competitors do not take unfair advantage. He wants to help you do your best.

2) Listen to all instructions

Don't jump the gun! Wait until you understand all directions. In most civil service tests you get more time than you need to answer the questions. So don't be in a hurry. Read each word of instructions until you clearly understand the meaning. Study the examples, listen to all announcements and follow directions. Ask questions if you do not understand what to do.

3) Identify your papers

Civil service exams are usually identified by number only. You will be assigned a number; you must not put your name on your test papers. Be sure to copy your number correctly. Since more than one exam may be given, copy your exact examination title.

4) Plan your time

Unless you are told that a test is a "speed" or "rate of work" test, speed itself is usually not important. Time enough to answer all the questions will be provided, but this does not mean that you have all day. An overall time limit has been set. Divide the total time (in minutes) by the number of questions to determine the approximate time you have for each question.

5) Do not linger over difficult questions

If you come across a difficult question, mark it with a paper clip (useful to have along) and come back to it when you have been through the booklet. One caution if you do this – be sure to skip a number on your answer sheet as well. Check often to be sure that you have not lost your place and that you are marking in the row numbered the same as the question you are answering.

6) Read the questions

Be sure you know what the question asks! Many capable people are unsuccessful because they failed to *read* the questions correctly.

7) Answer all questions

Unless you have been instructed that a penalty will be deducted for incorrect answers, it is better to guess than to omit a question.

8) Speed tests

It is often better NOT to guess on speed tests. It has been found that on timed tests people are tempted to spend the last few seconds before time is called in marking answers at random – without even reading them – in the hope of picking up a few extra points. To discourage this practice, the instructions may warn you that your score will be "corrected" for guessing. That is, a penalty will be applied. The incorrect answers will be deducted from the correct ones, or some other penalty formula will be used.

9) Review your answers

If you finish before time is called, go back to the questions you guessed or omitted to give them further thought. Review other answers if you have time.

10) Return your test materials

If you are ready to leave before others have finished or time is called, take ALL your materials to the monitor and leave quietly. Never take any test material with you. The monitor can discover whose papers are not complete, and taking a test booklet may be grounds for disqualification.

VIII. EXAMINATION TECHNIQUES

1) Read the general instructions carefully. These are usually printed on the first page of the exam booklet. As a rule, these instructions refer to the timing of the examination; the fact that you should not start work until the signal and must stop work at a signal, etc. If there are any *special* instructions, such as a choice of questions to be answered, make sure that you note this instruction carefully.

2) When you are ready to start work on the examination, that is as soon as the signal has been given, read the instructions to each question booklet, underline any key words or phrases, such as *least, best, outline, describe* and the like. In this way you will tend to answer as requested rather than discover on reviewing your paper that you *listed without describing*, that you selected the *worst* choice rather than the *best* choice, etc.

3) If the examination is of the objective or multiple-choice type – that is, each question will also give a series of possible answers: A, B, C or D, and you are called upon to select the best answer and write the letter next to that answer on your answer paper – it is advisable to start answering each question in turn. There may be anywhere from 50 to 100 such questions in the three or four hours allotted and you can see how much time would be taken if you read through all the questions before beginning to answer any. Furthermore, if you come across a question or group of questions which you know would be difficult to answer, it would undoubtedly affect your handling of all the other questions.

4) If the examination is of the essay type and contains but a few questions, it is a moot point as to whether you should read all the questions before starting to answer any one. Of course, if you are given a choice – say five out of seven and the like – then it is essential to read all the questions so you can eliminate the two that are most difficult. If, however, you are asked to answer all the questions, there may be danger in trying to answer the easiest one first because you may find that you will spend too much time on it. The best technique is to answer the first question, then proceed to the second, etc.

5) Time your answers. Before the exam begins, write down the time it started, then add the time allowed for the examination and write down the time it must be completed, then divide the time available somewhat as follows:
    - If 3-1/2 hours are allowed, that would be 210 minutes. If you have 80 objective-type questions, that would be an average of 2-1/2 minutes per question. Allow yourself no more than 2 minutes per question, or a total of 160 minutes, which will permit about 50 minutes to review.
    - If for the time allotment of 210 minutes there are 7 essay questions to answer, that would average about 30 minutes a question. Give yourself only 25 minutes per question so that you have about 35 minutes to review.

6) The most important instruction is to *read each question* and make sure you know what is wanted. The second most important instruction is to *time yourself properly* so that you answer every question. The third most important instruction is to *answer every question*. Guess if you have to but include something for each question. Remember that you will receive no credit for a blank and will probably receive some credit if you write something in answer to an essay question. If you guess a letter – say "B" for a multiple-choice question – you may have guessed right. If you leave a blank as an answer to a multiple-choice question, the examiners may respect your feelings but it will not add a point to your score. Some exams may penalize you for wrong answers, so in such cases *only*, you may not want to guess unless you have some basis for your answer.

7) Suggestions
    a. Objective-type questions
        1. Examine the question booklet for proper sequence of pages and questions
        2. Read all instructions carefully
        3. Skip any question which seems too difficult; return to it after all other questions have been answered
        4. Apportion your time properly; do not spend too much time on any single question or group of questions

5. Note and underline key words – *all, most, fewest, least, best, worst, same, opposite*, etc.
6. Pay particular attention to negatives
7. Note unusual option, e.g., unduly long, short, complex, different or similar in content to the body of the question
8. Observe the use of "hedging" words – *probably, may, most likely*, etc.
9. Make sure that your answer is put next to the same number as the question
10. Do not second-guess unless you have good reason to believe the second answer is definitely more correct
11. Cross out original answer if you decide another answer is more accurate; do not erase until you are ready to hand your paper in
12. Answer all questions; guess unless instructed otherwise
13. Leave time for review

  b. Essay questions
1. Read each question carefully
2. Determine exactly what is wanted. Underline key words or phrases.
3. Decide on outline or paragraph answer
4. Include many different points and elements unless asked to develop any one or two points or elements
5. Show impartiality by giving pros and cons unless directed to select one side only
6. Make and write down any assumptions you find necessary to answer the questions
7. Watch your English, grammar, punctuation and choice of words
8. Time your answers; don't crowd material

8) Answering the essay question

Most essay questions can be answered by framing the specific response around several key words or ideas. Here are a few such key words or ideas:

M's: manpower, materials, methods, money, management
P's: purpose, program, policy, plan, procedure, practice, problems, pitfalls, personnel, public relations

  a. Six basic steps in handling problems:
1. Preliminary plan and background development
2. Collect information, data and facts
3. Analyze and interpret information, data and facts
4. Analyze and develop solutions as well as make recommendations
5. Prepare report and sell recommendations
6. Install recommendations and follow up effectiveness

  b. Pitfalls to avoid
1. *Taking things for granted* – A statement of the situation does not necessarily imply that each of the elements is necessarily true; for example, a complaint may be invalid and biased so that all that can be taken for granted is that a complaint has been registered

2. *Considering only one side of a situation* – Wherever possible, indicate several alternatives and then point out the reasons you selected the best one
3. *Failing to indicate follow up* – Whenever your answer indicates action on your part, make certain that you will take proper follow-up action to see how successful your recommendations, procedures or actions turn out to be
4. *Taking too long in answering any single question* – Remember to time your answers properly

IX. AFTER THE TEST

Scoring procedures differ in detail among civil service jurisdictions although the general principles are the same. Whether the papers are hand-scored or graded by machine we have described, they are nearly always graded by number. That is, the person who marks the paper knows only the number – never the name – of the applicant. Not until all the papers have been graded will they be matched with names. If other tests, such as training and experience or oral interview ratings have been given, scores will be combined. Different parts of the examination usually have different weights. For example, the written test might count 60 percent of the final grade, and a rating of training and experience 40 percent. In many jurisdictions, veterans will have a certain number of points added to their grades.

After the final grade has been determined, the names are placed in grade order and an eligible list is established. There are various methods for resolving ties between those who get the same final grade – probably the most common is to place first the name of the person whose application was received first. Job offers are made from the eligible list in the order the names appear on it. You will be notified of your grade and your rank as soon as all these computations have been made. This will be done as rapidly as possible.

People who are found to meet the requirements in the announcement are called "eligibles." Their names are put on a list of eligible candidates. An eligible's chances of getting a job depend on how high he stands on this list and how fast agencies are filling jobs from the list.

When a job is to be filled from a list of eligibles, the agency asks for the names of people on the list of eligibles for that job. When the civil service commission receives this request, it sends to the agency the names of the three people highest on this list. Or, if the job to be filled has specialized requirements, the office sends the agency the names of the top three persons who meet these requirements from the general list.

The appointing officer makes a choice from among the three people whose names were sent to him. If the selected person accepts the appointment, the names of the others are put back on the list to be considered for future openings.

That is the rule in hiring from all kinds of eligible lists, whether they are for typist, carpenter, chemist, or something else. For every vacancy, the appointing officer has his choice of any one of the top three eligibles on the list. This explains why the person whose name is on top of the list sometimes does not get an appointment when some of the persons lower on the list do. If the appointing officer chooses the second or third eligible, the No. 1 eligible does not get a job at once, but stays on the list until he is appointed or the list is terminated.

X. HOW TO PASS THE INTERVIEW TEST

The examination for which you applied requires an oral interview test. You have already taken the written test and you are now being called for the interview test – the final part of the formal examination.

You may think that it is not possible to prepare for an interview test and that there are no procedures to follow during an interview. Our purpose is to point out some things you can do in advance that will help you and some good rules to follow and pitfalls to avoid while you are being interviewed.

What is an interview supposed to test?

The written examination is designed to test the technical knowledge and competence of the candidate; the oral is designed to evaluate intangible qualities, not readily measured otherwise, and to establish a list showing the relative fitness of each candidate – as measured against his competitors – for the position sought. Scoring is not on the basis of "right" and "wrong," but on a sliding scale of values ranging from "not passable" to "outstanding." As a matter of fact, it is possible to achieve a relatively low score without a single "incorrect" answer because of evident weakness in the qualities being measured.

Occasionally, an examination may consist entirely of an oral test – either an individual or a group oral. In such cases, information is sought concerning the technical knowledges and abilities of the candidate, since there has been no written examination for this purpose. More commonly, however, an oral test is used to supplement a written examination.

Who conducts interviews?

The composition of oral boards varies among different jurisdictions. In nearly all, a representative of the personnel department serves as chairman. One of the members of the board may be a representative of the department in which the candidate would work. In some cases, "outside experts" are used, and, frequently, a businessman or some other representative of the general public is asked to serve. Labor and management or other special groups may be represented. The aim is to secure the services of experts in the appropriate field.

However the board is composed, it is a good idea (and not at all improper or unethical) to ascertain in advance of the interview who the members are and what groups they represent. When you are introduced to them, you will have some idea of their backgrounds and interests, and at least you will not stutter and stammer over their names.

What should be done before the interview?

While knowledge about the board members is useful and takes some of the surprise element out of the interview, there is other preparation which is more substantive. It *is* possible to prepare for an oral interview – in several ways:

1) Keep a copy of your application and review it carefully before the interview

This may be the only document before the oral board, and the starting point of the interview. Know what education and experience you have listed there, and the sequence and dates of all of it. Sometimes the board will ask you to review the highlights of your experience for them; you should not have to hem and haw doing it.

2) Study the class specification and the examination announcement

Usually, the oral board has one or both of these to guide them. The qualities, characteristics or knowledges required by the position sought are stated in these documents. They offer valuable clues as to the nature of the oral interview. For example, if the job involves supervisory responsibilities, the announcement will usually indicate that knowledge of modern supervisory methods and the qualifications of the candidate as a supervisor will be tested. If so, you can expect such questions, frequently in the form of a hypothetical situation which you are expected to solve. NEVER go into an oral without knowledge of the duties and responsibilities of the job you seek.

3) Think through each qualification required

Try to visualize the kind of questions you would ask if you were a board member. How well could you answer them? Try especially to appraise your own knowledge and background in each area, *measured against the job sought*, and identify any areas in which you are weak. Be critical and realistic – do not flatter yourself.

4) Do some general reading in areas in which you feel you may be weak

For example, if the job involves supervision and your past experience has NOT, some general reading in supervisory methods and practices, particularly in the field of human relations, might be useful. Do NOT study agency procedures or detailed manuals. The oral board will be testing your understanding and capacity, not your memory.

5) Get a good night's sleep and watch your general health and mental attitude

You will want a clear head at the interview. Take care of a cold or any other minor ailment, and of course, no hangovers.

What should be done on the day of the interview?

Now comes the day of the interview itself. Give yourself plenty of time to get there. Plan to arrive somewhat ahead of the scheduled time, particularly if your appointment is in the fore part of the day. If a previous candidate fails to appear, the board might be ready for you a bit early. By early afternoon an oral board is almost invariably behind schedule if there are many candidates, and you may have to wait. Take along a book or magazine to read, or your application to review, but leave any extraneous material in the waiting room when you go in for your interview. In any event, relax and compose yourself.

The matter of dress is important. The board is forming impressions about you – from your experience, your manners, your attitude, and your appearance. Give your personal appearance careful attention. Dress your best, but not your flashiest. Choose conservative, appropriate clothing, and be sure it is immaculate. This is a business interview, and your appearance should indicate that you regard it as such. Besides, being well groomed and properly dressed will help boost your confidence.

Sooner or later, someone will call your name and escort you into the interview room. *This is it.* From here on you are on your own. It is too late for any more preparation. But remember, you asked for this opportunity to prove your fitness, and you are here because your request was granted.

What happens when you go in?

The usual sequence of events will be as follows: The clerk (who is often the board stenographer) will introduce you to the chairman of the oral board, who will introduce you to the other members of the board. Acknowledge the introductions before you sit down. Do not be surprised if you find a microphone facing you or a stenotypist sitting by. Oral interviews are usually recorded in the event of an appeal or other review.

Usually the chairman of the board will open the interview by reviewing the highlights of your education and work experience from your application – primarily for the benefit of the other members of the board, as well as to get the material into the record. Do not interrupt or comment unless there is an error or significant misinterpretation; if that is the case, do not hesitate. But do not quibble about insignificant matters. Also, he will usually ask you some question about your education, experience or your present job – partly to get you to start talking and to establish the interviewing "rapport." He may start the actual questioning, or turn it over to one of the other members. Frequently, each member undertakes the questioning on a particular area, one in which he is perhaps most competent, so you can expect each member to participate in the examination. Because time is limited, you may also expect some rather abrupt switches in the direction the questioning takes, so do not be upset by it. Normally, a board member will not pursue a single line of questioning unless he discovers a particular strength or weakness.

After each member has participated, the chairman will usually ask whether any member has any further questions, then will ask you if you have anything you wish to add. Unless you are expecting this question, it may floor you. Worse, it may start you off on an extended, extemporaneous speech. The board is not usually seeking more information. The question is principally to offer you a last opportunity to present further qualifications or to indicate that you have nothing to add. So, if you feel that a significant qualification or characteristic has been overlooked, it is proper to point it out in a sentence or so. Do not compliment the board on the thoroughness of their examination – they have been sketchy, and you know it. If you wish, merely say, "No thank you, I have nothing further to add." This is a point where you can "talk yourself out" of a good impression or fail to present an important bit of information. Remember, *you close the interview yourself*.

The chairman will then say, "That is all, Mr. _____, thank you." Do not be startled; the interview is over, and quicker than you think. Thank him, gather your belongings and take your leave. Save your sigh of relief for the other side of the door.

How to put your best foot forward

Throughout this entire process, you may feel that the board individually and collectively is trying to pierce your defenses, seek out your hidden weaknesses and embarrass and confuse you. Actually, this is not true. They are obliged to make an appraisal of your qualifications for the job you are seeking, and they want to see you in your best light. Remember, they must interview all candidates and a non-cooperative candidate may become a failure in spite of their best efforts to bring out his qualifications. Here are 15 suggestions that will help you:

1) Be natural – Keep your attitude confident, not cocky

If you are not confident that you can do the job, do not expect the board to be. Do not apologize for your weaknesses, try to bring out your strong points. The board is interested in a positive, not negative, presentation. Cockiness will antagonize any board member and make him wonder if you are covering up a weakness by a false show of strength.

2) Get comfortable, but don't lounge or sprawl

Sit erectly but not stiffly. A careless posture may lead the board to conclude that you are careless in other things, or at least that you are not impressed by the importance of the occasion. Either conclusion is natural, even if incorrect. Do not fuss with your clothing, a pencil or an ashtray. Your hands may occasionally be useful to emphasize a point; do not let them become a point of distraction.

3) Do not wisecrack or make small talk

This is a serious situation, and your attitude should show that you consider it as such. Further, the time of the board is limited – they do not want to waste it, and neither should you.

4) Do not exaggerate your experience or abilities

In the first place, from information in the application or other interviews and sources, the board may know more about you than you think. Secondly, you probably will not get away with it. An experienced board is rather adept at spotting such a situation, so do not take the chance.

5) If you know a board member, do not make a point of it, yet do not hide it

Certainly you are not fooling him, and probably not the other members of the board. Do not try to take advantage of your acquaintanceship – it will probably do you little good.

6) Do not dominate the interview

Let the board do that. They will give you the clues – do not assume that you have to do all the talking. Realize that the board has a number of questions to ask you, and do not try to take up all the interview time by showing off your extensive knowledge of the answer to the first one.

7) Be attentive

You only have 20 minutes or so, and you should keep your attention at its sharpest throughout. When a member is addressing a problem or question to you, give him your undivided attention. Address your reply principally to him, but do not exclude the other board members.

8) Do not interrupt

A board member may be stating a problem for you to analyze. He will ask you a question when the time comes. Let him state the problem, and wait for the question.

9) Make sure you understand the question

Do not try to answer until you are sure what the question is. If it is not clear, restate it in your own words or ask the board member to clarify it for you. However, do not haggle about minor elements.

10) Reply promptly but not hastily

A common entry on oral board rating sheets is "candidate responded readily," or "candidate hesitated in replies." Respond as promptly and quickly as you can, but do not jump to a hasty, ill-considered answer.

11) Do not be peremptory in your answers

A brief answer is proper – but do not fire your answer back. That is a losing game from your point of view. The board member can probably ask questions much faster than you can answer them.

12) Do not try to create the answer you think the board member wants

He is interested in what kind of mind you have and how it works – not in playing games. Furthermore, he can usually spot this practice and will actually grade you down on it.

13) Do not switch sides in your reply merely to agree with a board member

Frequently, a member will take a contrary position merely to draw you out and to see if you are willing and able to defend your point of view. Do not start a debate, yet do not surrender a good position. If a position is worth taking, it is worth defending.

14) Do not be afraid to admit an error in judgment if you are shown to be wrong

The board knows that you are forced to reply without any opportunity for careful consideration. Your answer may be demonstrably wrong. If so, admit it and get on with the interview.

15) Do not dwell at length on your present job

The opening question may relate to your present assignment. Answer the question but do not go into an extended discussion. You are being examined for a *new* job, not your present one. As a matter of fact, try to phrase ALL your answers in terms of the job for which you are being examined.

Basis of Rating

Probably you will forget most of these "do's" and "don'ts" when you walk into the oral interview room. Even remembering them all will not ensure you a passing grade. Perhaps you did not have the qualifications in the first place. But remembering them will help you to put your best foot forward, without treading on the toes of the board members.

Rumor and popular opinion to the contrary notwithstanding, an oral board wants you to make the best appearance possible. They know you are under pressure – but they also want to see how you respond to it as a guide to what your reaction would be under the pressures of the job you seek. They will be influenced by the degree of poise you display, the personal traits you show and the manner in which you respond.

ABOUT THIS BOOK

This book contains tests divided into Examination Sections. Go through each test, answering every question in the margin. We have also attached a sample answer sheet at the back of the book that can be removed and used. At the end of each test look at the answer key and check your answers. On the ones you got wrong, look at the right answer choice and learn. Do not fill in the answers first. Do not memorize the questions and answers, but understand the answer and principles involved. On your test, the questions will likely be different from the samples. Questions are changed and new ones added. If you understand these past questions you should have success with any changes that arise. Tests may consist of several types of questions. We have additional books on each subject should more study be advisable or necessary for you. Finally, the more you study, the better prepared you will be. This book is intended to be the last thing you study before you walk into the examination room. Prior study of relevant texts is also recommended. NLC publishes some of these in our Fundamental Series. Knowledge and good sense are important factors in passing your exam. Good luck also helps. So now study this Passbook, absorb the material contained within and take that knowledge into the examination. Then do your best to pass that exam.

EXAMINATION SECTION

EXAMINATION SECTION
TEST 1

DIRECTIONS: Each question or incomplete statement is followed by several suggested answers or completions. Select the one that *BEST* answers the question or completes the statement. *PRINT THE LETTER OF THE CORRECT ANSWER IN THE SPACE AT THE RIGHT.*

1. Generally, the *MAIN* reason for using the questioning technique in a case work interview is to

    A. reveal discrepancies in information given by the client
    B. reinforce your own ideas about the case
    C. obtain necessary factual information about the client
    D. bring out the hidden motives of the client

    1.____

2. According to a basic case work principle, a worker should "accept" the client, regardless of the client's feelings, attitudes and behavior. This concept of "acceptance" means, most nearly, that the worker

    A. agrees with what the client says, does, and feels
    B. demonstrates his respect for the client as a human being
    C. has no strong opinions about the client's values
    D. thinks the way the client thinks

    2.____

3. Before visiting a new client, it is desirable for you to be prepared in advance, when possible.
    Which one of the following should generally NOT be included in these advance preparations?

    A. *Learning* as much as possible about the client from the medical chart
    B. *Trying* to put yourself in the client's place
    C. *Recognizing* your own prejudices and stereotypes
    D. *Deciding* on a solution to the client's problems

    3.____

4. After introducing yourself to a new patient, which one of the following questions generally would be the *MOST* appropriate for you to ask?

    A. "Do you expect any visitors today?"
    B. "Who is your attending physician?"
    C. "How can I be of help to you?"
    D. "Do you have hospitalization insurance?"

    4.____

5. In the middle of an interview, a patient makes a statement which seems unclear. Of the following, the *BEST* way to deal with this situation would be for the worker to

    A. ask the patient to rephrase her statement
    B. rephrase the statement, and ask the patient if that is what she meant
    C. inform the patient that she is not making herself clear
    D. let the patient finish and then try to tie the story together

    5.____

6. Assume that, at the conclusion of an interview with a client, you have reviewed problems that have been resolved. Generally, the MOST appropriate of the following closing actions for you to take would be to

   A. remind the patient to be on time for the next appointment
   B. go over specific actions that you and the client will take before the next visit
   C. remind the client to take tranquilizers when feeling upset
   D. ask the client to think of new problems to discuss during the next visit

7. Which one of the following would be a MAJOR responsibility of a worker assigned to the surgery ward?

   A. *Instructing* the nurse about changes in medication for patients
   B. *Advising* relatives of the best time to visit patients
   C. *Detecting* anxiety of patients due to their medical illness
   D. *Recording* the number of visitors received by patients

8. Assume that you have been assigned the case of an eight-year-old child whose parents were both seriously injured in an automobile accident. You realize that this child will have severe problems in the months ahead.
   During the *first* interview, of the following, the BEST way to assist the child would be to

   A. convince the child of his ability to be brave and grown-up
   B. play a competitive game with the child and let him win
   C. help the child express his fears and reassure him in accordance with reality
   D. tell the child that his problems are not so great as they may seem

9. Assume that one of your clients has many medical and social problems and needs a good deal of supportive case work help.
   Which one of the following approaches would generally be MOST appropriate for you to use in order to help this client cope with these problems?

   A. *Try* to make the client feel that his problems and situation are unique
   B. *Encourage* the client to be realistic about his situation and assure him that you understand and will do everything possible to help him cope
   C. *Emphasize* to the client those areas you feel you can work on and those which you can do nothing about
   D. *Urge* the client to refrain from taking action on serious matters without asking for your help first

10. Assume that, when you discuss with one of your elderly clients the advisability of applying to the department of socital services for financial assistance, the client becomes extremely upset about the prospect of having to be interviewed by "another stranger."
    Of the following, the BEST way to handle this situation would be to

    A. explain that applying for financial assistance is something the client must do by herself and for herself
    B. offer to accompany the client to social services if necessary, and work with the client toward greater future independence
    C. withdraw your suggestion, since the client's emotional health is your primary consideration
    D. suggest that the client take a personal friend to the interview to help with difficult questions, if necessary

11. Assume that a newspaper reporter calls and questions you regarding the long wait for treatment in the Emergency Room. Of the following, your MOST appropriate response would be to

    A. advise the reporter that the long wait is caused by an enormous increase in emergency cases
    B. refer the reporter to the director of social work
    C. tell the reporter that your hospital's emergency room is one of the most efficient in the city
    D. refer the reporter to the hospital employee responsible for public relations

12. When a worker interviews a patient whose problem seems to be typical of that of many other patients she has seen, of the following, it would be MOST appropriate to

    A. *attempt* to learn more about the individual circumstances of this patient's situation
    B. *handle* this case the same way as the others were handled
    C. *ask* another worker how she generally handles this type of problem
    D. *reassure* the patient by telling him that many other patients have similar problems

13. A patient without friends or relatives is being discharged from the hospital. He complains to you that his shoes are missing.
    Of the following, your MOST appropriate response would be to

    A. advise the patient that this is not a professional concern of yours and suggest that he speak to the ward nurse
    B. advise the patient that he will have to buy a pair of shoes from a nearby shoe store
    C. obtain a pair of shoes for the patient in the hospital clothing room
    D. tell the patient that he probably was not wearing shoes at the time he was admitted

14. The parents of a hospitalized child complain to you that their child is not getting proper nursing care. You have ample opportunity to observe what is happening on the pediatric ward and know that the nurses are extremely conscientious in caring for the children. Your *initial* interpretation of this complaint should be that, probably, the parents

    A. are projecting their anxiety about the child's health by criticizing the nurses
    B. are chronic complainers and must be treated accordingly
    C. may actually want to transfer the child to a more conveniently located hospital
    D. are trying to get special treatment for their child from the nurses

15. You are interviewing an unmarried, attractive young female patient who was in an automobile accident and will not be able to walk again. She says to you: "I'll never find a husband now that I'm crippled."
    In order to help her express her feelings freely, of the following, your MOST appropriate response would be:

    A. "You feel that no one will marry you because you can't walk."
    B. "Don't be silly. You have your whole life ahead of you."
    C. "That's not necessarily true. You're young and pretty and smart."
    D. "That may be true, but at least you're alive."

16. Assume that you are in your office completing some paperwork. A man enters and introduces himself as a close friend of one of your patients in the terminal cancer ward. He then asks if he can speak with you, and sits down in the chair next to your desk.
    Of the following, it would be MOST appropriate for you to say FIRST:

    A. "You probably want to know how your friend is coping with his condition."
    B. "You realize, of course, that your friend is dying of cancer."
    C. "What would you like to see me about?"
    D. "What problem would you like to discuss?"

17. During an interview with a new patient your mind wanders momentarily, and you have missed some details in the patient's story.
    Which one of the following would be most appropriate to say FIRST, before the patient continues?

    A. "And then what happened?" – so that the patient will think that you were paying attention all along.
    B. "Could you rephrase that?" – so that the patient will restate the details without being aware of your inattentiveness.
    C. "I'm sorry, I didn't get that, could you repeat that part?" – so that the patient will perceive you as an honest person.
    D. "Please continue". – so that the patient will not have to repeat something that was probably unimportant anyway.

18. Assume that one of your clients is telling you about her family situation. All of a sudden, she says: "Two of my kids go to school, and the third, who is seventeen, ..."
    Then she stops speaking.
    In this situation, of the following, it would be most appropriate for you to FIRST

    A. state: "works?"
    B. state: "quit school?"
    C. ask: "What about the third child?"
    D. remain silent for a few seconds

19. You have just started to interview a new client. He begins by telling you that he has been unemployed for the past three years and is receiving almost as much from welfare as he did when he was working. He continues talking along these lines, and then asks you why anybody would want to work when they can be on the dole and maintain almost the same standard of living.
    Of the following, your MOST appropriate response would be:

    A. "I don't personally approve of living in that manner."
    B. "It all depends on a person's values and standards."
    C. "If you are happy living like that, it's all right with me."
    D. "Let's not discuss that. Let's talk about your medical problems first."

20. During your second interview with a young woman, she asks you to drop all this professional stuff and just be friends.
Which one of the following would be your appropriate response?

    A. "If we were friends, I would probably not be so effective in helping you deal with your problem."
    B. "That's O.K. with me, but you would have to be reassigned to a different worker."
    C. "That would be impossible under the rules and regulations of our agency."
    D. "I really don't think that's appropriate, and I'm a very busy person."

20.____

KEY (CORRECT ANSWERS)

1.	C	11.	D
2.	B	12.	A
3.	D	13.	C
4.	C	14.	A
5.	A	15.	A
6.	B	16.	C
7.	C	17.	C
8.	C	18.	D
9.	B	19.	B
10.	B	20.	A

TEST 2

DIRECTIONS: Each question or incomplete statement is followed by several suggested answers or completions, Select the one that *BEST* answers the question or completes the statement. *PRINT THE LETTER OF THE CORRECT ANSWER IN THE SPACE AT THE RIGHT.*

1. You are interviewing a young man who confides, in you that he is now on probation. In order to help this patient, you decide that it would be desirable to contact his probation officer to obtain additional information.
   Of the following, the BEST way to contact the probation officer would be

   A. *after* the interview, with the patient's consent
   B. *after* the interview, without the patient's consent
   C. *after* the interview, without telling the patient
   D. *during* the interview, with the patient present

   1.____

2. You introduce yourself to a newly-hospitalized patient and offer to be of assistance if possible. The patient nods that she understands, and begins to discuss her 12-year-old daughter's truancy from school.
   Which one of the following responses would be most appropriate for you to make FIRST?

   A. *I understand your daughter's problem, but can we discuss your problems now?*
   B. *How do you feel this will affect you while you are in the hospital?*
   C. *Did your daughter fail any of her subjects because of her truancy?*
   D. *I have a very large caseload today. Perhaps we can discuss your daughter another time.*

   2.____

3. You have been interviewing a patient for almost an hour and it is time for your next appointment. As you are about to finish, the patient begins to discuss a new problem.
   In this situation, it would generally be advisable to

   A. close the interview and make another appointment with the patient to discuss this problem
   B. allow the patient to *get things off his chest* before closing the interview
   C. ask the patient why he brought this problem up at the last moment
   D. tell the patient that you cannot discuss this problem because you will be late for your next appointment

   3.____

4. Assume that you are completing a case involving a deteriorating relationship between the parents of a child who was hospitalized due to an accident caused by the child's father. Since counselling began upon admission of the child, there has been a marked improvement in the relationship between the parents and, in particular, between the child and the father. The child is about to be discharged from the hospital, and you are having an interview with the parents.
   Of the following, according to accepted casework practice, it would be MOST appropriate for you to

   A. assure the parents that, as a result of counselling, they are now *ideal* parents
   B. offer a continuation of counselling until the family's adjustment is stable
   C. review with the parents the *do's and don'ts* of being *good* parents
   D. explain to the parents how you helped them solve their problems

   4.____

5. Assume that one of your clients, an adult male out-patient who has been coming to see you weekly for four months, fails to keep two appointments. The physician informs you that one of this patient's laboratory tests is positive, indicating the urgent need for follow-up medical care. You have sent the patient a telegram, but he has not replied after a reasonable length of time.
According to accepted casework practice, of the following, the MOST advisable action for you to take would be to

   A. *contact* a neighbor of the patient and ask the neighbor to persuade the patient to return to the hospital
   B. *inform* a member of the patient 's family of the positive; test result and emphasize the urgency of the situation
   C. *write* to the patient and explain the dangers of not returning to the hospital for treatment
   D. *make* an emergency visit to the patient at home and tell him about the positive test result and the importance of returning to the hospital

6. Assume that you are trying to establish the identity of an elderly woman who was brought to the Emergency Room by the police, who found her on the street, somewhat disoriented. The doctor decides to admit the woman, whose blood pressure is elevated, and who has an open ulcerated wound on her leg. She is very talkative about events long in the past, can't recall where she lives, but keeps speaking of having to *go home to give her sister breakfast*. The police have found that she has a card giving her name and an address which is three blocks from the hospital, but the telephone company has no listing for her.
Of the following, your MOST advisable action would be to

   A. ask the hospital security guards to make a visit to the address on the card and tell any relatives of the woman that she is hospitalized
   B. have a visiting nurse make a visit to the address and check on the sister's possible need for food and medical attention
   C. call the social service exchange to determine whether the woman is known to any agency and what information they may have about her and her sister
   D. make a visit to the address on the card in order to obtai more information about the woman

7. You are a worker assigned to the alcoholism clinic. One of your clients appears for an interview in an intoxicated condition. Of the following, your MOST appropriate action would be to

   A. discuss the patient's drinking problem with him in no uncertain terms
   B. make another appointment and point out to the patient that he cannot be interviewed while intoxicated
   C. threaten to close the case and discharge the patient if he does not sober up
   D. recommend psychological testing to determine why the patient persists in drinking in spite of counselling

8. As a worker in the family planning clinic, you are counselling an 18-year-old unmarried patient who is pregnant. She is in a state of conflict, because she wants an abortion, but her boyfriend is encouraging her to marry him and bear the child.
Of the following, your MOST appropriate action would be to

   A. ask the patient why she was careless after receiving guidance from the family planning clinic
   B. encourage the patient to make the decision for herself, and Be supportive of her choice
   C. stress the positive qualities of her boyfriend, who is offering to marry her
   D. determine whether the conflict may derive from the patient's religious upbringing

9. Assume that one of your cases, a woman who has given birth three days ago, is now verbally abusive to the staff, and refuses to see her infant. Of the following, your MOST appropriate course of action would be to

   A. scold the woman for her childish behavior
   B. attempt to convince the woman that once she sees the baby she will feel much better
   C. speak with the woman in an effort to understand her behavior
   D. tell the woman that she will be transferred to the psychiatric unit if she does not behave

10. Assume that you are interviewing an unmarried female patient in the Emergency Room. The doctor has just told her that she must be admitted to the hospital on an emergency basis, but she refuses to accept this recommendation because she has three small children, has no one to care for them, and does not want to leave them alone.
Of the following, the most appropriate action for you to take FIRST would be to

    A. suggest that the patient try to enlist neighbors to help look after the children
    B. ask the doctor to admit the children with their mother on an emergency basis
    C. try to locate the children's father and ask him to look after the children
    D. explain to the patient that it is possible for you to arrange for care of the children

11. Assume that you are assigned to the methadone maintenance clinic. As you are about to finish an interview, your client asks you to lend him ten dollars. Of the following, your most appropriate FIRST action would be to

    A. inform the client that it is against hospital policy for a worker to lend money to a patient
    B. lend the client the ten dollars
    C. suggest that the client borrow the money from a personal friend
    D. advise the client to apply to the department of social services for an emergency grant

12. You are interviewing a young unmarried woman who is pregnant, says that she is not sure she can care for her baby properly, and is considering requesting an abortion. Of the following, your MOST appropriate response would be:

    A. *What do you think of as proper care for your baby?*
    B. *I'm sure you will be an excellent mother.*
    C. *Do you know who the father is?*
    D. *How long have you been pregnant?*

13. You are interviewing a married patient with two young children with regard to her impending surgery. Suddenly, she asks if you are married. Of the following, the MOST appropriate response would be to tell her

    A. whether you are married, and then ask why she wants to know
    B. you are not now married, but that you are engaged to be married
    C. this is irrelevant, and continue discussing her situation
    D. you used to be married, but that you are now divorced

14. You are visiting a new patient on your assigned ward. After introducing yourself and offering to be of assistance, the patient begins to tell you a lengthy story relating to her illness. According to accepted interviewing techniques, of the following, it would be MOST appropriate for you to indicate your concern and interest by

    A. briefly commenting or asking questions, indicating that you are grasping the essential points
    B. saying nothing, so as not to interrupt the patient's train of thought
    C. interrupting frequently to clarify points you do not fully comprehend
    D. asking the patient to pause at periodic intervals so that you may proceed to ask structured questions

15. You have been counseling an adult patient on the cancer ward on a weekly basis for about a month and it is now time to decide where the patient will live after being discharged from the hospital.
    According to accepted practice, the FINAL decision on this matter should be made by

    A. you, the case worker
    B. the patient's relatives
    C. the patient, with the case worker's help
    D. the patient and the doctors

16. Assume that a patient in your caseload asks you for specific advice regarding his unhappy marital situation. In deciding whether to respond to this request, you should generally consider all of the following EXCEPT

    A. any possible underlying anxiety the patient may have
    B. the patient's ability to carry out the advice
    C. the seriousness of the patient's situation
    D. whether the client will accept or reject your advice

17. According to accepted casework practice, when interviewing a young child it is considered especially important for the worker to closely observe the child's behavior, feelings, and mood, in addition to listening to what the child says, MAINLY because such observation should

    A. provide significant diagnostic information about the child
    B. help the child feel closer to the worker
    C. enable the worker to sense the right time to console the child
    D. give the worker clues as to when to humor the child

18. You find it necessary to refer a client for psychiatric help upon discharge. The client consents to this plan, but asks you to omit from your report certain information he has told you in confidence. You feel that the psychiatrist's knowledge of this information would be of great benefit in helping your client.
    For you to go ahead and include this information in your report to the psychiatrist, without the client's consent, would be considered

    A. *good practice*, because the psychiatrist will need all available information about the client
    B. *bad practice*, because this action would be a breach of confidence
    C. *good practice*, because helping the client is the primary goal of case work
    D. *bad practice,* because the patient would probably find out eventually that this information was disclosed

19. You are interviewing a woman who has suffered a severe beating from her husband, is obviously upset, and embarrassed about having to relate the details to you.
    Of the following, the MOST appropriate way for you to handle this situation would be to

    A. insist that she tell you the whole story, including the details
    B. postpone discussion of the beating until the woman feels better
    C. tell the woman to omit the details for now, and ask her how you can be of help
    D. postpone this interview until the husband is available to present his side of the story

20. You are making discharge plans for an alert, 78-year-old retired school teacher who is recovering satisfactorily from a minor operation. One day, when you come to her room, she fails to recognize you and tells you disconnected stories about people she knew in childhood.
    Of the following, the MOST appropriate way to handle this changed situation would be to

    A. tell the patient she had better *snap out of it*
    B. advise the patient that you will return when she starts talking sense
    C. confer with the attending physician about this change in the patient's condition
    D. suggest to the physician that the discharge plan be changed to recommend admission to a State hospital

KEY (CORRECT ANSWERS)

1.	A	11.	A
2.	B	12.	A
3.	A	13.	A
4.	B	14.	A
5.	D	15.	C
6.	D	16.	D
7.	B	17.	A
8.	B	18.	B
9.	C	19.	C
10.	D	20.	C

EXAMINATION SECTION
TEST 1

DIRECTIONS: Each question or incomplete statement is followed by several suggested answers or completions. Select the one that BEST answers the question or completes the statement. *PRINT THE LETTER OF THE CORRECT ANSWER IN THE SPACE AT THE RIGHT.*

1. As a worker in the outpatient clinic, you are helping a patient complete a Medicaid application. Although he appears to be eligible, the patient is reluctant to give the information necessary to complete the application.
   Of the following, your MOST appropriate action in this situation would be to
   A. inform your supervisor that the patient is uncooperative and request permission to close the case
   B. advise the patient that he cannot be seen in the clinic again unless the application is completed
   C. discuss with the patient the reasons for his reluctance to apply for medical assistance
   D. explain to the patient that the bill will be turned over to a collection agency if the Medicaid application is not completed

    1.____

2. You have been counseling a long-term patient once a week for several weeks. However, due to a reorganization in your hospital's department of social work, this patient will be assigned to another worker within three weeks.
   Of the following, the MOST appropriate time to tell the patient about the change in workers is
   A. immediately to give you time to help the patient adjust to the idea of another worker
   B. at the time of the new worker's first visit, to avoid any possible resentment by the patient towards you
   C. at the beginning of your final visit, to allow time to tell the patient what you know about the new worker
   D. at the end of your final visit, to avoid a possible sentimental farewell scene

    2.____

3. As you enter the clinic area where you are assigned as a worker, you see an elderly man trip and fall on the curb near the doorway. Which one of the following actions should you take FIRST?
   A. Inform the executive director about this accident.
   B. Assist the man to his feet and help him into the clinic area so that he can be more comfortable.
   C. Stay with the man and tell him not to move while you ask someone to summon help.
   D. Go to the nearest phone and call the police.

    3.____

4. Which one of the following health service systems would generally be suitable for a chronically ill or disabled patient who has had an acute episode or a relapse at home?
   A. Skilled nursing home
   B. General hospital
   C. Extended care facility
   D. Home attendant service

   4.____

5. Assume that you are trying to arrange placement for an elderly patient who, upon discharge from the hospital, will be able to get around and manage by herself, but will require some supervision.
   Of the following, the MOST appropriate placement for this patient would be in a
   A. nursing home
   B. rehabilitation center
   C. chronic care facility
   D. health-related facility

   5.____

6. Assume that you are helping an elderly patient with discharge planning. This patient, who is expected to live alone in his own apartment, will need around-the-clock assistance with personal needs, such as bathing and taking of medication.
   Of the following services, the one that should be recommended for this patient is a
   A. homemaker
   B. housekeeper
   C. home attendant
   D. visiting nurse

   6.____

7. You are counseling an elderly woman who lives alone. You and the doctor have decided that she requires nursing home placement upon discharge from the hospital. However, the woman has expressed fear and concern about being uprooted from her home and living among strangers.
   In this situation, the BEST of the following courses of action would be to
   A. try to convince the woman that a nursing home is best
   B. allow the woman to make her own decision, after offering her advice and guidance
   C. recommend that the woman be permitted to live in her own home and manage as best she can
   D. ask the woman's doctor to encourage her to accept nursing home placement

   7.____

Questions 8-10.

DIRECTIONS: Questions 8 through 10 are to be answered on the basis of the information given in the following case record.

Laura Jackson
Age: 52
Single
Parents – Deceased
Sibling: Sister – Sally Mays, age 53, married
Diagnosis: Multiple Sclerosis

Ms. Jackson, a high school graduate, supported herself as a salesclerk since graduation, but continued to live at home with her parents until their sudden death in an automobile accident 13 years ago. Since that time, she lived alone, but had continual contact with her older sister, Mrs. Sally Mays. A year ago, Ms. Jackson's hand became too unsteady for her to work. This condition had been preceded by forgetfulness and frequent mistakes. Examinations resulted in a diagnosis of multiple sclerosis, and she became increasingly incapacitated until she had difficulty feeding and dressing herself. After a very serious fall, Ms. Jackson was hospitalized.

The case worker, together with Mrs. Mays, arranged for Ms. Jackson to be placed in a nursing home in anticipation of her discharge from the hospital. She would be unable to care for herself alone at home, and her sister could not take care of her because of household responsibilities. Ms. Jackson is extremely unhappy and angry when she is told about the decision to place her in a nursing home. She accuses her sister of plotting to put her away. Mrs. Mays turns to the case worker for advice.

8. On the basis of the above information, of the following, the circumstance which would help explain Ms. Jackson's anger when she was told about being placed in a nursing home is that she
   A. is probably becoming paranoid as a result of her illness
   B. has undoubtedly actively disliked her sister for years
   C. was not involved in the process of making the decision
   D. was a dependent person before she became ill

9. When Mrs. Mays turns to the case worker for advice after recognizing her sister's anger, of the following, it would be MOST appropriate for the case worker to FIRST
   A. reassure Mrs. Mays that she has made the best decision for Ms. Jackson's care
   B. tell Mrs. Mays that you will visit Ms. Jackson and calm her down
   C. help Mrs. Mays to understand why Ms. Jackson is upset
   D. ask Mrs. Mays to visit Ms. Jackson and explain why the decision was made

10. Of the following, the MOST important factor to consider in finding a nursing home for Ms. Jackson is
    A. the ratio of men to women among the patients
    B. a location that will make it possible for Mrs. Mays to visit frequently
    C. her need for a single room, since she has always lived alone
    D. the average age of the other patients

11. Assume that, when you discuss with one of your elderly clients the advisability of applying to the department of social services for financial assistance, the client becomes extremely upset about the prospect of having to be interviewed by another stranger.
    Of the following, the BEST way to handle this situation would be to
    A. explain that applying for financial assistance is something the client must do by herself and for herself
    B. offer to accompany the client to social services if necessary and work with the children toward greater future independence

C. withdraw your suggestion since the client's emotional health is your primary consideration
D. suggest that the client take a personal friend to the interview to help with difficult questions, if necessary

12. Assume that you are trying to establish the identity of an elderly woman who was brought to the emergency room by the police, who found her on the street, somewhat disoriented. The doctor decides to admit the woman, whose blood pressure is elevated and who has an open ulcerated wound on her leg. She is very talkative about events long in the past, can't recall where she lives, but keeps speaking of having to *go home to give her sister breakfast*. The police have found that she has a card giving her name and an address which is three blocks from the hospital, but the telephone company has no listing for her.
Of the following, your MOST advisable action would be to
    A. ask the hospital security guards to make a visit to the address on the card and tell any relatives of the woman that she is hospitalized
    B. have a visiting nurse make a visit to the address and check on the sister's possible need for food and medical attention
    C. call the social service exchange to determine whether the woman is known to any agency and what information they may have about her and her sister
    D. make a visit to the address on the card in order to obtain more information about the woman

13. You are making discharge plans for an alert, 78-year-old retired school teacher who is recovering satisfactorily from a minor operation. One day, when you come to her room, she fails to recognize you and tells you disconnected stories about people she knew in childhood.
Of the following, the MOST appropriate way to handle this changed situation would be to
    A. tell the patient she had better *snap out of it*
    B. advise the patient that you will return when she starts talking sense
    C. confer with the attending physician about this change in the patient's condition
    D. suggest to the physician that the discharge plan be changed to recommend admission to a state hospital

14. If a patient is repeatedly admitted to the hospital because of a series of mishaps in which he has suffered broken bones, the one of the following which is MOST likely to be true is that he is
    A. a rigid person   B. a diabetic   C. malingering
    D. accident-prone   E. psychotic

15. The one of the following groups of illnesses which is known to be caused by bacteria is
    A. mental diseases   B. acute infectious diseases
    C. nutritional diseases   D. degenerative diseases
    E. cancerous tumors

16. The one of the following with which Hodgkin's disease is COMMONLY associated is
    A. neurasthenia   B. meningitis   C. poliomyelitis
    D. cancer   E. tuberculosis

17. The one of the following diseases in which the determination of the sedimentation rate is important for diagnostic purposes is
    A. rheumatic heart disease   B. congenital heart disease
    C. hypertensive heart disease   D. diabetes
    E. gonorrhea

18. The one of the following disease classifications which would include spinal meningitis is
    A. cancer or tumor   B. nutritional disease
    C. acute infectious disease   D. focal or local infection
    E. acute poisoning or intoxication

19. The one of the following diseases which may cause visual impairment and blindness is
    A. ringworm   B. osteomyelitis
    C. poliomyelitis   D. gall bladder disease
    E. diabetes

20. The one of the following which is NOT an anesthetic is
    A. cholesterol   B. nitrous oxide
    C. sodium pentothal   D. procaine
    E. ethyl chloride

21. The one of the following which BEST describes the restrictions to be applied to Mr. K., a cardiac patient classified, according to the standards of the American Heart Association, as Functional, Class IV D, is
    A. limited activity
    B. complete bed rest
    C. four hours rest daily
    D. prohibition of stair climbing, alcohol, or tobacco
    E. convalescent status

22. Geriatrics is becoming an increasingly important branch of medicine. Of the following, this is CHIEFLY due to
    A. greater specialization within the medical profession
    B. the discovery of penicillin and aureomycin
    C. advances in medical eduction
    D. increases in hospitalization
    E. the increase in the span of life

23. Morbidity rate refers to the
    A. incidence of an illness
    B. ratio of births to deaths
    C. bacterial count
    D. degree of disability caused by an illness
    E. death rate

24. One day an elderly man asks you if he can apply for Social Security at the welfare office. Your response should be to
    A. tell him that it is foolish to think he can apply for Social Security at the welfare office
    B. take him back to his apartment because he is too old to be roaming the streets asking questions
    C. explain that Social Security is a federal program and direct him to the nearest Social Security office
    D. call his daughter and tell her that the family should take better care of their father

25. The area senior citizens group asks for an agency representative to discuss old-age assistance and new SSI regulations. Your supervisor asks you to attend this meeting; however, you do not wish to go because you really do not feel that you work well with older people. In fact, you don't like them very much.
    What should be your response?
    A. Tell the supervisor that you cannot go because you have an appointment with the doctor that day
    B. Get another worker to go for you and assume his task while he is gone
    C. Explain to your supervisor what problems you have in working with old-age clients
    D. Go, because you should do the tasks that are assigned to you according to your job description

26. A man being interviewed is entitled to Medicaid, but he refuses to sign up for it because he says he cannot accept any form of welfare.
    Of the following, the BEST course of action for an aide to take FIRST is
    A. try to discover the reason for his feeling this way
    B. tell him that he should be glad financial help is available
    C. explain that others cannot help him if he will not help himself
    D. suggest that he speak to someone who is already on Medicaid

27. Miss Lally is an old-age assistance recipient. Her health is not good, and it is important that she have three good meals each day. She follows these instructions except on Friday she refuses to eat meat because of her religious beliefs. She will not even substitute fish. You are very concerned about this, so you should
    A. tell your supervisor so that she will go to see Miss Lally and make her eat nourishing meals on Friday
    B. call her doctor and tell him so that he will see her and explain to her that fasting is not good for her health

C. attempt to understand her value system and accept that it is possible that she is acting in good faith with her own values, even though they may be harmful to her health
D. explain to her how important it is that she eat meat each day in order to be in good health and enjoy the remaining years of her life

28. In working with community groups, it is important that you be able to define what a community is. Of the following definitions, which is the MOST appropriate?
A community
   A. consists of a group of people living fairly close together in a more or less compact territory, who come together in their chief concerns
   B. is a particular section of a city designated on a census tract
   C. is that portion of a city which constitutes an election district
   D. is a section of a city or town in which a particular ethnic group conducts its social, business, and religious life

29. New regulations have removed the disabled, blind, and old-age assistance cases from the public assistance caseload. Assistance in these categories is given directly by the federal government. A former client has not received his check. The chairman of the senior citizens committee calls and angrily demands that your agency do something in this man's behalf.
In response, you should
   A. answer politely, explaining that your agency is not concerned about OAA clients
   B. arrange to meet with him in order to discuss the new policy
   C. refer him to the Social Security office covering the area where the client lives
   D. ask that he call again when he is calmer so that you may discuss this matter with him

30. The MOST practical method of maintaining income for the majority of aged persons who are no longer able to work, or for the families of those workers who are deceased, is a(n)
   A. comprehensive system of non-categorical assistance on a basis of cash payments
   B. integrated system of public assistance and extensive work relief programs
   C. system of contributory insurance in which a cash benefit is paid as a matter of right
   D. expanded system of diagnostic and treatment centers

KEY (CORRECT ANSWERS)

1.	C	11.	B	21.	B
2.	A	12.	D	22.	E
3.	C	13.	C	23.	A
4.	B	14.	D	24.	C
5.	D	15.	B	25.	C
6.	C	16.	D	26.	A
7.	A	17.	A	27.	C
8.	C	18.	C	28.	A
9.	C	19.	E	29.	C
10.	B	20.	A	30.	D

TEST 2

DIRECTIONS: Each question or incomplete statement is followed by several suggested answers or completions. Select the one that BEST answers the question or completes the statement. *PRINT THE LETTER OF THE CORRECT ANSWER IN THE SPACE AT THE RIGHT.*

1. With the establishment of insurance and assistance programs under the Social Security Act, many institutional programs for the aged have tended to the greatest extent toward an increased emphasis on providing, of the following types of assistance,
    A. care for the aged by denominational groups
    B. care for children requiring institutional treatment
    C. recreational facilities for the able-bodied aged
    D. training facilities in industrial homework for the aged
    E. care for the chronically ill and infirm aged

    1.____

2. Of the following terms, the one which BEST describes the Social Security Act is
    A. enabling legislation
    B. regulatory statute
    C. appropriations act
    D. act of mandamus
    E. provisional enactment

    2.____

3. A typical characteristic of the United States population over 65 is that MOST of them
    A. are independent and capable of self-support
    B. live in their own homes but require various supportive services
    C. live in institutions for the aged
    D. require constant medical attention at home or in an institution

    3.____

4. The one of the following factors which is MOST important in preventing persons 65 years of age and older from getting employment is the
    A. misconceptions by employers of skills and abilities of senior citizens
    B. lack of skill in modern industrial techniques of persons in this age group
    C. Social Security laws restricting employment of persons in this age group
    D. unwillingness of persons in this age group to continue supporting themselves

    4.____

5. A sponge rubber mattress will help to prevent pressure sores because it exerts
    A. pressure only on the extremities
    B. no pressure on the heavier parts of the body
    C. no pressure on the body
    D. equal pressure on all parts of the body

    5.____

6. A physiological change in vision common in old age results in
    A. farsightedness
    B. nearsightedness
    C. double vision
    D. lack of coordination

    6.____

7. Salt is restricted in a cardiac diet because salt will 7.____
   A. promote retention of fluid in the tissues
   B. decreases the permeability of the blood cell membrane
   C. impair the elasticity of the blood vessels
   D. cling to the lining of the blood vessels

8. Salts may exert a diuretic effect because they are 8.____
   A. excreted as solutes   B. irritating to the urinary bladder
   C. absorbed rapidly   D. dehydrating

9. In the administration of oxygen, moisture is added to the oxygen to reduce the 9.____
   A. fire hazard
   B. water evaporation from mucous membranes
   C. surface tension
   D. kindling temperature

10. The CORRECT body alignment for a patient lying on the side is with the 10.____
    A. head in a straight line with the spine and knees slightly flexed
    B. shoulders rotated slightly forward and head tipped forward
    C. torso in a straight line and legs extended
    D. shoulders straight, legs extended, and head tipped slightly backward

11. If a patient shows signs of a pressure sore at the base of the spine, the home nurse should 11.____
    A. try a sitting position for the patient
    B. use small cotton wings on the pressure spot
    C. apply an ointment to the sore
    D. place an air-ring under the patient's buttocks

12. The purpose of a plaster cast is to 12.____
    A. produce traction   B. reduce the fracture
    C. immobile the bone   D. straighten the bone

13. In lifting a patient from a low plane, the nurse should NOT 13.____
    A. lower her own center of gravity
    B. flex her own knees
    C. exert the patient's weight against her vertebral axis
    D. keep her own feet together

14. If a patient lying on her side is uncomfortable, the nurse may give her a(n) 14.____
    A. extra top cover
    B. snug abdominal bandage
    C. back rest
    D. pillow to support the lumbar region

15. The diet for a patient with gallstones may include 15.____
    A. grapefruit juice   B. liver
    C. cream   D. peas

16. A rich source of vitamin K is
    A. butter   B. spinach   C. oranges   D. milk

17. Flaxseed meal is prescribed for making an application of moist heat because of its
    A. medicinal properties
    B. mucilaginous ingredients
    C. lightness
    D. ability to retain heat

18. In cardiac disease, the purpose of the low sodium diet is to
    A. relieve edema
    B. increase kidney function by changing the salt balance
    C. reduce weight through decrease of appetite
    D. make sure that the patient is salt free

19. Of the following, the procedure which violates a law of physics and increases fatigue is
    A. working with the patient in center of bed
    B. carrying a basin of water close to the body
    C. carrying a basin by placing palms flat around the sides
    D. standing with feet apart

20. The explanation of the fact that the comfort of the patient is related to the height of the headrest is: The _____ the headrest, the greater the _____.
    A. higher; distribution of body weight
    B. lower; distribution of body weight
    C. lower; strain on the sacrum
    D. lower; pressure on the buttocks

21. Decubitus ulcers in bed-ridden patients are BEST avoided by the use of
    A. plasticized rings
    B. rubberized terry cotton draw sheets
    C. sheepskin
    D. polyurethane foam

22. The aged citizen is BEST cared for in
    A. the home environment
    B. old age homes
    C. hospitals for the aged
    D. a town developed for old people

23. An ailment found ONLY in older people is
    A. manic depression
    B. dementia praecox
    C. senile dementia
    D. tabes dorsalis

24. The outstanding change, of the following, in the aging process is that the aged are
    A. irritable
    B. no longer self-reliant
    C. senile
    D. easily influenced by stress

25. Re-adjusting the older person to be somewhat self-sufficient is known as
    A. stabilization
    B. regeneration
    C. rejuvenation
    D. rehabilitation

26. MOST prone to accidents in the home is the
    A. young adult
    B. middle-aged individual
    C. adolescent
    D. aged individual

27. In general, the sleep requirement for an aged person as compared to the sleep requirement for a young adult is
    A. less
    B. more
    C. the same
    D. slightly greater

28. A factor which contributes to wrinkling of the skin in the aged is
    A. hydration of tissues
    B. decrease in pigmentation
    C. loss of elasticity
    D. increase in calcium deposits

29. Diseases associated with the aged are assuming increasing importance. One of these chronic conditions the nurse frequently finds is acute cerebral thrombosis with resulting hemiplegia.
    To bring about MAXIMUM rehabilitation, the nurse should assist in a program in which
    A. the patient is encouraged to help himself only when, and if, he feels he is able to do so
    B. the patient is immobilized until the acute phase is over and the patient is able to start to help himself
    C. any portion of the body is prevented from remaining in a position of flexion long enough to permit muscle shortening to occur
    D. the use of the affected muscles and the opposing muscles is discouraged for at least four weeks following the onset of illness

30. A voluntary agency which has pioneered in gerontology is
    A. Young Men's Christian Association
    B. The Salvation Army
    C. The Union Health Center
    D. The Community Service Society

KEY (CORRECT ANSWERS)

1.	E	11.	D	21.	D
2.	A	12.	C	22.	A
3.	B	13.	D	23.	C
4.	A	14.	D	24.	D
5.	D	15.	A	25.	D
6.	A	16.	B	26.	D
7.	A	17.	D	27.	A
8.	A	18.	A	28.	C
9.	B	19.	A	29.	C
10.	A	20.	B	30.	D

EXAMINATION SECTION
TEST 1

DIRECTIONS: Each question or incomplete statement is followed by several suggested answers or completions. Select the one that BEST answers the question or completes the statement. *PRINT THE LETTER OF THE CORRECT ANSWER IN THE SPACE AT THE RIGHT.*

1. The one of the following diseases which is the LEADING cause of death in the 10-to-15 year age group is
 A. cancer
 B. tuberculosis
 C. poliomyelitis
 D. diabetes
 E. rheumatic fever

 1.____

2. The one of the following which would MOST likely be a result of untreated syphilis is
 A. paresis
 B. phlebitis
 C. carcinoma
 D. silicosis
 E. angina pectoris

 2.____

3. The one of the following which is MOST likely to be used in establishing a diagnosis of epilepsy is a(n)
 A. electrocardiogram
 B. spinal x-ray
 C. fluoroscopic examination
 D. electroencephalogram
 E. psychometric examination

 3.____

4. The pathology of diabetes involves the FAILURE of the body to produce an adequate supply of
 A. sugar
 B. carbohydrates
 C. insulin
 D. salt
 E. bile

 4.____

5. The one of the following statements that is TRUE about diabetes is that
 A. it can generally be cured if medical orders are followed
 B. it can generally be kept under control but not cured
 C. it is an infectious disease
 D. blindness is an inevitable result of it
 E. controlled diabetes is a progressively disabling disease

 5.____

6. Scurvy is caused by a deficiency of vitamin
 A. A
 B. B
 C. C
 D. E
 E. K

 6.____

7. Vitamin D deficiency is common because
 A. it can only be injected
 B. it is generally associated with poorly tasting foods
 C. only physicians can administer it
 D. it is not found naturally in many foods

 7.____

8. The one of the following vitamins that is used as an aid in coagulating blood is vitamin
 A. A
 B. B
 C. C
 D. E
 E. K

 8.____

9. The one of the following statements that is TRUE of Duchenne muscular dystrophy is that
    A. it is transmitted to the male children through the mother
    B. the male is the carrier of the disease
    C. the brain is primarily affected because of a lack of blood supply
    D. it is caused by a nutritional deficiency in the antepartum period
    E. only female children are susceptible to the disease

10. If a patient is repeatedly admitted to the hospital because of a series of mishaps in which he has suffered broken bones, the one of the following that is MOST likely to be true is that he is
    A. a rigid person   B. a diabetic   C. malingering
    D. accident prone   E. psychotic

11. The one of the following groups of illnesses that is known to be caused by bacteria is
    A. mental diseases
    B. acute infectious diseases
    C. nutritional diseases
    D. degenerative diseases
    E. cancerous tumors

12. The one of the following with which Hodgkin's Disease is COMMONLY associated is
    A. neurasthenia   B. meningitis   C. poliomyelitis
    D. cancer   E. tuberculosis

13. The one of the following diseases in which the determination of the sedimentation rate is IMPORTANT for diagnostic purposes is
    A. rheumatic heart disease   B. congenital heart disease
    C. hypertensive heart disease   D. diabetes
    E. gonorrhea

14. The one of the following disease classifications that would INCLUDE spinal meningitis is
    A. cancer or tumor   B. nutritional disease
    C. acute infectious disease   D. focal or local infection
    E. acute poisoning or intoxication

15. The one of the following diseases that may cause visual impairment and blindness is
    A. ringworm   B. osteomyelitis
    C. poliomyelitis   D. gall bladder disease
    E. diabetes

16. The one of the following that is NOT an anesthetic is
    A. cholesterol   B. nitrous oxide   C. sodium pentothal
    D. procaine   E. ethyl chloride

17. The one of the following that BEST describes the restrictions to be applied to Mr. K., a cardiac patient classified, according to the standards of the American Heart Association, as functional, Class IVD, is
    A. limited activity
    B. complete bed rest
    C. four hours rest daily
    D. prohibition of stair climbing, alcohol or tobacco
    E. convalescent status

    17.____

18. Over time, geriatrics has become an increasingly important branch of medicine CHIEFLY due to
    A. greater specialization within the medical profession
    B. the discovery of penicillin and aureomycin
    C. advances in medical education
    D. increases in hospitalization
    E. the increase in the span of life

    18.____

19. The one of the following which is MOST likely to be an occupational disease is
    A. cancer
    B. cerebral hemorrhage
    C. septicemia
    D. asthma
    E. nephritis

    19.____

20. The one of the following that is a NUTRITIONAL disease is
    A. tuberculosis   B. scurvy   C. hepatitis
    D. lymphoma   E. scabies

    20.____

21. Morbidity rate refers to the
    A. incidence of an illness
    B. ratio of births to deaths
    C. bacterial count
    D. degree of disability caused by an illness
    E. death rate

    21.____

22. A pediatrician is a doctor who specializes in the treatment of
    A. children   B. foot diseases
    C. disabling illnesses   D. orthopedic diseases
    E. the aged

    22.____

23. A sadistic person is one who
    A. receives gratification through suffering pain
    B. secures a great deal of satisfaction from his own body
    C. receives gratification from inflicting pain on others
    D. turns all feelings towards others back into his own personality
    E. seeks solace through deep mental depression

    23.____

24. The one of the following which is said to be the masculine counterpart of the *Electra Complex* is the _____ complex.
    A. sexual perversion   B. frustration   C. Oedipus
    D. reanimation   E. repression

    24.____

25. The one of the following conditions for which a patient would be admitted to a state mental hospital is
    A. schizophrenia
    B. muscular dystrophy
    C. pathological lying
    D. congenital syphilis
    E. psychoneurosis

26. The one of the following statements which BEST describes the difference between a hallucination and a delusion is that
    A. hallucinations occur only at night
    B. delusions occur only with menopause
    C. delusions are primarily provoked by sexual function
    D. a hallucination has a basis in beliefs or ideas
    E. a delusion has a basis in beliefs or ideas

27. Finger sucking in early childhood has long been a subject of discussion among psychiatrists.
    The one of the following statements that is GENERALLY accepted as true is that
    A. finger sucking denotes pending neuroses and the parents need psychiatric consultation
    B. finger sucking is a normal activity of early childhood and should not be interfered with
    C. finger sucking alters the child's facial contours and should be heavily discouraged
    D. finger sucking by a child over nine months old is due to emotional upset and needs treatment
    E. the physician should discuss possible remedial measures such as guards on fingers

28. The one of the following who is said to be the *Father of Medicine* is
    A. Hippocrates
    B. Pasteur
    C. Galen
    D. Sydenham
    E. Plato

29. The one of the following who is credited with the improvement of conditions in mental hospitals and the founding of new ones in the United States is
    A. Andrew Jackson
    B. Dorothea Dix
    C. William Knowlton
    D. Robert Stack
    E. Rene Laennec

30. The one of the following doctors whose name is COMMONLY associated with much of the early growth and subsequent progress of medical social work is Dr.
    A. Sigmund Freud
    B. Richard C. Cabot
    C. Elizabeth Blackwell
    D. Carmyn Lombardo
    E. Thomas Parran

KEY (CORRECT ANSWERS)

1.	A	11.	B	21.	A
2.	A	12.	D	22.	A
3.	D	13.	A	23.	C
4.	C	14.	C	24.	C
5.	B	15.	E	25.	A
6.	C	16.	A	26.	E
7.	D	17.	B	27.	B
8.	E	18.	E	28.	A
9.	A	19.	D	29.	B
10.	D	20.	B	30.	B

EXAMINATION SECTION
TEST 1

DIRECTIONS: Each question or incomplete statement is followed by several suggested answers or completions. Select the one that BEST answers the question or completes the statement. *PRINT THE LETTER OF THE CORRECT ANSWER IN THE SPACE AT THE RIGHT.*

1. A medical social worker can give service to an incurably ill patient MOST effectively by

    A. urging him to sleep and rest a great deal to conserve his strength
    B. helping him to gain what satisfaction he can within the limits imposed by his illness
    C. instructing his family to give him everything he asks for
    D. limiting her visits to him so she will not tire him

   1.____

2. A SOUND motive for entering the field of social work is a desire to

    A. satisfy a personal need for giving
    B. be in a position to dispense charity
    C. accumulate information concerning the behavior of maladjusted people
    D. help people whose lives are unhappy or without satisfaction

   2.____

3. The one of the following which is of MOST value to a social case worker in carrying out her functions in any field of social work is a(n)

    A. full knowledge of community resources
    B. totally objective viewpoint toward hostile behavior
    C. awareness of the purposeful use of relationships
    D. mature personality free from conflicts

   3.____

4. The social case worker, in giving help to a client, should use PRIMARILY

    A. the community facilities available to meet needs
    B. the resources of the patient and his immediate environment
    C. the agency policies to determine her focus
    D. psychiatric concepts of human behavior

   4.____

5. A case worker who is new to the field of social work will MOST probably focus her efforts PRIMARILY on

    A. the problem as presented by the client
    B. the client in relation to his problem
    C. developing self-awareness in handling clients
    D. the emotional needs of the client

   5.____

6. A social worker who cannot adhere to agency policies is MOST likely to be a person who

    A. cannot relate to people
    B. has problems centered around questions of authority
    C. has deep feelings of guilt
    D. has many domestic problems

   6.____

7. The one of the following cases which a beginning social case worker would probably find the LEAST difficult to handle is one involving a(n)

    A. juvenile delinquent
    B. enuretic child
    C. normal child in need of convalescent care
    D. stuttering child

8. A social worker can BEST begin to help a couple with a marital problem by FIRST

    A. referring them to a psychiatrist
    B. referring them to the family physician for guidance
    C. suggesting that they go to court with their problem
    D. helping them to clarify for themselves the nature of their problem

9. The social case worker often finds that legally responsible relatives of her clients are hostile when expected to contribute towards support or payment of medical expenses of the client.
The one of the following which would be the MOST desirable way of dealing with such hostility is for the social worker to

    A. look into her own background to understand why these relatives are so resistant
    B. tell the relatives that this is a legal responsibility which cannot be evaded
    C. suggest that the relatives contact their legislators toward changing this requirement
    D. acknowledge the hardships involved for relatives and give understanding and treatment of the problem involved

10. A medical social work consultant from the Crippled Children's Bureau, in helping to set up a program of convalescent care for long-term orthopedically crippled patients, should prefer foster home care to institutional care PRIMARILY because

    A. a greater degree of emotional security would thereby be provided
    B. the children could then attend public school with normal children
    C. medical care of the children would then be better
    D. the families could then visit the children more frequently

11. The one of the following statements in regard to the emotional needs and attitudes of children which is MOST accurate is that

    A. it is not possible for a working mother to meet the emotional needs of her child
    B. parents who receive public assistance cannot meet the child's need for security
    C. a child who is emotionally secure does not have feelings of aggression
    D. parental support and acceptance are important to develop a feeling of belonging in the child

12. Persistent feeding problems with nursery or school-age children are MOST probably caused by

    A. hostility toward the mother
    B. the physical make-up of the child
    C. impoverished home conditions
    D. basic personality maladjustments

13. Local health departments and crippled children's agencies are assuming more and more responsibility for the teaching of various professional groups. Medical social workers are participating actively in programs of educational institutions and in-service training.
    The CHIEF objective of such teaching by a medical social worker is to

    A. supplement the knowledge of other professional groups so that they may perform minor case work services for the patient group
    B. teach social work concepts and demonstrate the need for more extensive medical social work
    C. encourage each professional group to realize fully the need of understanding every individual
    D. bring to other professions an approach to medical social work techniques which can be integrated into their own practice

14. The provision of medical services by the Department of Social Services for its recipients is presently and has been in the past

    A. focused on rehabilitation through employment
    B. all-inclusive to meet the needs of the clients
    C. supplementary to other community health services
    D. focused primarily on the medical needs of adults

15. Assume that a child who is a ward of the Foundling Hospital and who has been in a foster home placement through that agency is admitted to a city hospital with acute appendicitis.
    The required consent for an operation MUST be obtained from the

    A. hospital superintendent   B. foster parent
    C. Foundling Hospital   D. next of kin

16. The one of the following which is the MOST important point for a medical social worker to stress in the initial orientation of a group of new case workers to the use of agency case records is the

    A. statistical use of the records
    B. confidentiality of the material
    C. value of records in court
    D. type of recording used

4 (#1)

17. When a medical social worker in a hospital is requested to assist with the teaching of medical students, it is a CARDINAL principle that the meetings must 17.____

   A. be attended by either the supervisor or the director of the social service division
   B. be held at the hospital to give meaning to the students
   C. be sponsored by the clinical teacher of the students
   D. have a patient present for demonstration purposes

18. An employee in a social agency who is charged with administrative functions should 18.____

   A. carry personal liability insurance
   B. make his opinions subordinate to those of his staff members
   C. be willing to delegate authority
   D. make decisions regarding all matters of policy without consulting his staff members

19. In interpreting agency function and administrative structure to a group of case workers, it is important to point out that policies are set up PRIMARILY to 19.____

   A. define the duties of each worker
   B. limit the amount of expenditures
   C. obtain state or federal reimbursement
   D. provide help for client and worker

20. Consultation in social work is MOST effective when the consultee 20.____

   A. understands that such consultation is an administrative order
   B. has a set schedule for consultation conferences
   C. recognizes his need for help and requests it
   D. recognizes the superior intelligence of the consultant

Questions 21-25.

DIRECTIONS: In Questions 21 through 25, Column I lists titles of books and Column II lists authors. Select the author for each book listed in Column I and write the letter which precedes the author in the blank space at the right, which corresponds to the number of the question.

COLUMN I	COLUMN II	
21. SUPERVISION IN SOCIAL CASE WORK	A. Edith Abbott	21.____
	B. Carol Cooley	
22. SOCIAL WELFARE AND PROFESSIONAL EDUCATION	C. Thomas Parran	22.____
	D. G. Canby Robinson	
23. SHADOW ON THE LAND; SYPHILIS	E. Virginia P. Robinson	23.____
24. THE MEANING OF DISEASE	F. Frances Upham	24.____
	G. William A. White	
25. SOCIAL ASPECTS OF ILLNESS		25.____

KEY (CORRECT ANSWERS)

1. B
2. D
3. C
4. B
5. A

6. B
7. C
8. D
9. D
10. A

11. D
12. D
13. D
14. C
15. C

16. B
17. C
18. C
19. D
20. C

21. E
22. A
23. C
24. G
25. B

TEST 2

DIRECTIONS: Each question or incomplete statement is followed by several suggested answers or completions. Select the one that BEST answers the question or completes the statement. *PRINT THE LETTER OF THE CORRECT ANSWER IN THE SPACE AT THE RIGHT.*

1. The federal government accepts a responsibility for promoting and stimulating a comprehensive health program for all our people.
   The CHIEF reason for the assumption of this responsibility is that

   A. the health of our people is probably our most important national resource
   B. in some of the states the morbidity and mortality rates are extremely high
   C. greater medical needs are emerging as the nation is getting to be *a nation of elders*
   D. the medical profession has been unable to cover the needs of the major portion of the population

   1.___

2. The medical profession was at first opposed to state legislation calling for mandatory reporting by doctors of certain contagious and communicable diseases to local health departments.
   Their resistance was based PRIMARILY on the fact that they believed that

   A. this law would cause them to lose their patients
   B. the individual was more important than society
   C. this law was a violation of medical ethics
   D. this law would lead to socialized medicine

   2.___

3. The state governments in the United States have traditionally assumed responsibility for caring for

   A. merchant seamen
   B. the mentally ill
   C. patients with contagious diseases
   D. victims of industrial accidents

   3.___

4. The one of the following organizations which is supported from public funds is the

   A. National Institution of Health
   B. American Public Welfare Association
   C. American Public Health Association
   D. National Council on Family Relations

   4.___

5. Prior to 1935, the federal government assumed medical responsibility CHIEFLY for

   A. widows and orphans   B. federal employees
   C. tuberculous patients   D. military personnel

   5.___

6. The one of the following programs of the Social Security Act which is DIRECTLY administered by the federal government through the Social Security Administration is

   A. old age and survivors' insurance
   B. aid to the disabled
   C. aid to crippled children
   D. old age assistance

   6.___

7. The Social Security Act authorizes funds to be allotted by the Children's Bureau to the states so that needed services can be made readily available to all crippled children in the state.
In actual practice,

   A. the eligibility of a child for care is determined only on basis of medical needs
   B. states determine eligibility for service on basis of economic as well as medical needs
   C. all patients with childhood crippling conditions are accepted for care
   D. the act restricts the types of crippling conditions for which services will be available

8. The one of the following which would cause an employee to be INELIGIBLE for state unemployment insurance benefits is

   A. possession of a private unemployment insurance policy
   B. loss of job because of termination of business by employer
   C. dismissal because of seasonal layoffs
   D. dismissal because of misconduct

9. Old age and survivors' insurance and workmen's compensation are similar in that they both

   A. require a *means* test to determine eligibility for benefits
   B. are concerned with benefit rights based on past employment
   C. operate under state administration with federal guidance
   D. require court action for determination of benefits

10. In the city, shelter care for children is provided by private agencies as well as the Children's Center. The private agencies are licensed by the

    A. Department of Health
    B. Department of Welfare
    C. Department of Hospitals
    D. State Department of Social Services

11. The licensing of nursing homes in the city is the responsibility of the

    A. Department of Health
    B. Department of Hospitals
    C. Department of Social Services
    D. State Department of Social Welfare

12. A public welfare agency differs from a private welfare agency in that the former functions within

    A. administrative rules
    B. budgetary requirements
    C. a framework of law
    D. a wider geographical unit

13. Legal incorporation of a private social agency is IMPORTANT because

    A. members of the staff will then avoid personal responsibility for acts of the agency
    B. it results in greater efficiency in running the agency
    C. the agency can then solicit funds without restrictions
    D. no other agency can then be set up to carry out the same functions

14. The one of the following agencies which will cover the cost of nursing home visits to a relief recipient who is on the home care program of a city hospital is the

    A. Department of Hospitals
    B. Department of Social Services
    C. Nursing Sisters of the Sick Poor
    D. Visiting Nurse Service

15. If a child of 15 years is stricken with poliomyelitis and needs braces for which his family cannot pay, the braces can be obtained through the

    A. State Division of Vocational Rehabilitation
    B. Department of Social Services
    C. Department of Hospitals
    D. Department of Health

16. The one of the following statements which is MOST accurate in regard to the employability clinics of the Department of Social Services which are located in city hospitals is that

    A. the hospital is partially reimbursed for services rendered
    B. the Department of Social Services is able to use the facilities of the hospitals without any payment
    C. only treatment of minor ailments is available in these clinics
    D. laboratory services for the clinics are supplied by the Department of Health

17. The state will reimburse the city for the cost of hospitalization of a person receiving aid to the blind to the extent of _____ percent of the total cost.

    A. 30   B. 50   C. 80   D. 100

18. The one of the following services which is FALSE is that

    A. the Department of Social Services maintains a panel of full-time salaried physicians who devote their services to treatment of the recipients
    B. an adult, with his or her consent, may be legally adopted by another adult
    C. any client of the Department of Social Services requiring examination to determine the degree of blindness may be examined at a Department of Social Services eye clinic
    D. no minor should be treated in a hospital or clinic without written consent of a parent or guardian

4 (#2)

19. The one of the following statements which is NOT true is that the Department of Social Services

    A. does not reimburse the Department of Hospitals for out-patient service given to its clients
    B. provides drugs for its clients who receive care in an out-patient clinic of a city hospital
    C. may provide appliances for a client attending an out-patient clinic of a city hospital
    D. will pay for a client's transportation to the outpatient clinic of a voluntary hospital

20. The one of the following statements in regard to the use of statistics in social work which is MOST valid is that

    A. statistics are non-essential to budget presentation
    B. statistics speak for themselves and need no interpretation
    C. uniformity of statistical controls is unimportant
    D. statistics are essential in planning the agency program

21. The one of the following which is the LEAST accurate statement in regard to the use of statistical controls in public welfare administration is that statistics

    A. furnish conclusive evidence as to the quality of the worker's performance
    B. are required by law
    C. are an indication of the employee's use of his time
    D. can serve as a supervisory tool for evaluation of work

22. The one of the following which is set up to further the control of alcoholism is

    A. Men's Shelter   B. William Hodson Center
    C. Camp LaGuardia   D. Bridge House

23. In the city, the administrative authority for carrying out the public program for physically handicapped children rests with the _____ Department of _____.

    A. city; Health   B. city; Social Services
    C. city; Hospitals   D. state; Social Services

24. Teaching case workers how to use community resources can BEST be done by

    A. group meetings
    B. planning field trips to several agencies
    C. relating the teaching to their own cases
    D. bringing speakers to the agency staff meetings

25. If a child of 17 whose family is receiving aid to dependent children needs orthodontia, this service will be provided by the Department of

    A. Education   B. Hospitals
    C. Social Services   D. Health

KEY (CORRECT ANSWERS)

1. A
2. C
3. B
4. A
5. D

6. A
7. B
8. D
9. B
10. A

11. B
12. C
13. A
14. A
15. D

16. B
17. B
18. A
19. B
20. D

21. A
22. D
23. A
24. C
25. D

TEST 3

DIRECTIONS: Each question or incomplete statement is followed by several suggested answers or completions. Select the one that BEST answers the question or completes the statement. *PRINT THE LETTER OF THE CORRECT ANSWER IN THE SPACE AT THE RIGHT.*

1. Assume that you are a medical social work consultant in the Department of Social Services, and a social investigator consults you about a client who refuses needed hospitalization. The investigator feels that the client should be pressured into accepting hospital care.
   The one of the following points which you should emphasize to the investigator is

   A. the desirability of getting relatives to sway the client towards accepting hospital care
   B. agency rules against the use of pressure
   C. the client's right of self-determination
   D. legal provisions against forcing the client to accept hospital care

2. The major part of the costs of medical care for persons receiving public assistance in the city is represented by

   A. hospital costs B. physicians' visits
   C. nurses' visits D. surgical appliances

3. The Public Health Law of the state was amended to change the provisions relating to charges and reimbursement for hospital care and treatment of persons with tuberculosis. The one of the following which is MOST accurate in regard to this amendment is that

   A. the state will reimburse each locality 100% for state charges in local tuberculosis hospitals
   B. the 50% state aid formula is changed to a maximum of $5 per patient day
   C. each locality is now responsible for the total cost of the care of its own residents in tuberculosis hospitals
   D. the state will assume full responsibility for the treatment and hospitalization of all diagnosed tuberculosis patients within the state

4. The services of a panel physician may not be authorized for clients of the Department of Social Services known to be suffering from

   A. an acute upper respiratory infection
   B. any contagious disease
   C. a chronic disease
   D. an acute form of venereal disease

5. In order to function most effectively as a medical social work consultant in the Department of Social Services, it would be important for the consultant to

   A. plan weekly conferences with the individual investigators around medical problems in their cases
   B. meet regularly on a scheduled basis with the unit supervisors to discuss cases with medical aspects
   C. review all the new cases each month for medical problems
   D. interview those clients who refuse to accept recommended medical care

41

6. In regard to the placement of clients of the Department of Social Services in nursing homes, the one of the following statements which is NOT true is that

   A. authorization by the medical director for nursing home care must be reviewed every three months
   B. assistance may be granted to residents of only those nursing homes which are approved by the Department of Social Services
   C. placement and residence in a nursing home must have the client's full consent and cooperation
   D. a plan for nursing home care requires the approval of the unit supervisor and the medical social work consultant

7. The medical care program in the Children's Center of the Department of Social Services is the direct responsibility of the Bureau of

   A. Child Welfare
   B. Social Services
   C. Institutional Administration
   D. Welfare Administration

Questions 8-11.

DIRECTIONS: Questions 8 through 11 are to be answered on the basis of the facts given in the case described below.

CASE I

Assume that you are a medical social work consultant in the Department of Social Services and a unit supervisor asks your assistance in the following case which is being carried by one of her investigators.

A young unmarried expectant mother from another city requests help with planning for herself and her baby. Except for one visit to a doctor to determine whether or not she was pregnant, she has had no prenatal care. She is without funds and has been evicted from her furnished room because of non-payment of rent. She is hesitant about giving information about herself because she does not wish her parents to know of her pregnancy. She has written to the father of her baby, who is a sergeant in the army, informing him of her pregnancy but has received no answer from him. She speaks vaguely of boarding the baby until she gets on her feet financially.

8. The one of the following which should be the social investigator's FIRST step in helping this girl is to

   A. offer her concrete help with her immediate problems, such as finding a place to live and planning for herself and her baby
   B. urge her to tell her parents so that they might help her
   C. discuss with her the advantages and disadvantages of boarding the baby or placing it for adoption
   D. offer to contact the baby's father through Red Cross

9. The one of the following agencies which would be LEAST likely to offer a helpful service to the client in this situation is the

   A. American Red Cross
   B. Department of Welfare
   C. St. Giles' Home
   D. Foundling Hospital

10. If this girl continues to be undecided about plans for her baby, the one of the following ways in which the social investigator could BEST help her is by

    A. suggesting that she get in touch with her parents so that she might have the benefit of their advice and counsel
    B. encouraging her to evaluate all possible plans and their advantages and disadvantages for the baby and for herself
    C. supporting her inclination to keep the baby and offering to help her find a foster home
    D. suggesting that she wait until she sees the baby before she considers plans

10.____

11. The one of the following ways in which the investigator could BEST help this girl to use this experience to make a more satisfactory adjustment to life in the future is by

    A. recognizing that she is lonely and referring her to recreational resources
    B. pointing out that unmarried mothers are neurotic and referring her to a psychiatrist
    C. helping her to use the interviews with the investigator to gain some self-understanding
    D. suggesting that the patient go home after the baby is born, since she appears to be unable to make a good adjustment away from her family and friends

11.____

Questions 12-20.

DIRECTIONS: Questions 12 through 20 are to be answered on the basis of the facts given in the case described below.

CASE II

Assume that in your capacity as a medical social work consultant in the Department of Social Services, the following situation is brought to your attention by a social investigator.

Mrs. G., a thirty-five year old Catholic woman, mother of three children and now pregnant, has been deserted by her husband and applies to the Department of Social Services for financial assistance. She says she does not know where her husband is. He had supported the family by working as a longshoreman until three months ago when he was discovered to have active tuberculosis. At that time, sanatorium care was recommended but he refused to go, and soon after he deserted his family.

Mrs. G. says her only living relatives are her step-mother, who lives with her, and two married step-brothers, living in the city, who have been helping her since Mr. G. deserted, but who now feel she should get help from the Department of Social Services. Mr. G.'s only relative is his mother, living in the city.

12. In abandoning his wife while she is pregnant, Mr. G. was LEGALLY guilty of

    A. a misdemeanor   B. a felony
    C. vagrancy   D. a fraud

12.____

13. The one of the following agencies which should be contacted FIRST in attempting to locate Mr. G. is the

    A. National Desertion Bureau
    B. Federal Bureau of Investigation
    C. Department of Social Services
    D. Police Department

13.____

14. If the Department of Social Services should be notified that Mr. G. is working in the city and able, but unwilling, to contribute to his family's support, the court where the department would start action is the _____ Court.

    A. Family Division of the Domestic Relations
    B. Children's Division of the Domestic Relations
    C. Criminal
    D. Supreme

15. If it is proved in this case that neither the father nor the mother is able to support the children, the LEGAL responsibility for the support of the children falls upon

    A. Mr. G.'s mother
    B. the Department of Social Services
    C. Mrs. G.'s step-mother
    D. Mrs. G.'s step-brothers

16. On the basis of Mrs. G.'s statement that her husband had active tuberculosis prior to his desertion, the social investigator on the case believes that each family member should be examined. The one of the following which would give DEFINITE evidence of active pulmonary tuberculosis in any of the family members is

    A. BCG vaccine   B. a Mantoux test
    C. a patch test   D. Roentgen study

17. The one of the following agencies to which you would refer the family for examination for tuberculosis is the

    A. nearest voluntary clinic
    B. State Tuberculosis and Health Association
    C. nearest city hospital
    D. Department of Health

18. If one of the children were found to have active pulmonary tuberculosis, the one of the following hospitals which would admit the child is _____ Hospital.

    A. St. Charles   B. Knickerbocker
    C. Seaview   D. Willowbrook

19. Mrs. G. shows concern about the care of her children during the period of her confinement. She states that if she goes to a hospital for delivery of her child, her step-mother would not be physically capable of giving them adequate care.
    In this situation, the one of the following plans which would be MOST adequate is to

    A. arrange home delivery
    B. plan for homemaker service
    C. place the children
    D. prove the step-mother's ability to care for the children

20. If Mrs. G. decides to go to a voluntary hospital clinic for prenatal care prior to delivery, the Department of Social Services will pay for

    A. medicines   B. laboratory fees
    C. x-ray examination   D. clinic fees

Questions 21-25.

DIRECTIONS: In Questions 21 through 25, Column I lists important happenings in the field of social welfare, and Column II lists dates. For each event listed in Column I, select its date from Column II, and write the letter which precedes the date in the space at the right corresponding to the number of the question.

	COLUMN I	COLUMN II	
21.	Enactment of the New York State Workmen's Compensation Law	A. 1875 B. 1910	21._____
22.	Enactment of the New York State Public Welfare Law	C. 1912 D. 1929	22._____
23.	Passage of the Social Security Act	E. 1931 F. 1933	23._____
24.	Establishment of the U.S. Children's Bureau	G. 1935	24._____
25.	Passage of the Federal Emergency Relief Act		25._____

KEY (CORRECT ANSWERS)

1. C   11. C
2. A   12. B
3. B   13. D
4. D   14. A
5. B   15. A

6. A   16. D
7. A   17. D
8. A   18. C
9. C   19. B
10. B 20. A

21. B
22. D
23. G
24. C
25. F

EXAMINATION SECTION
TEST 1

DIRECTIONS: Each question or incomplete statement is followed by several suggested answers or completions. Select the one that BEST answers the question or completes the statement. *PRINT THE LETTER OF THE CORRECT ANSWER IN THE SPACE AT THE RIGHT.*

1. Social case work is PRIMARILY

    A. a method of preventing juvenile delinquency
    B. the art of listening to others
    C. an interpretation to lay persons of social problems
    D. the determination of the individual's ability to meet situations
    E. an individual approach to people in trouble

2. Statistics show that the MAJORITY of people *initially* go to social agencies for

    A. recreational purposes
    B. help with financial problems
    C. vocational guidance
    D. help with marital problems
    E. help with emotional problems

3. Of the following, the trend followed by public welfare agencies at the present time is to

    A. give *relief in kind* to avoid wasteful spending of money
    B. give food and clothing vouchers on short–term cases
    C. discourage work relief projects
    D. give *cash relief* where the financial need has been established
    E. make public lists of relief recipients

4. In the initial interview with a client, the one of the following which is the MOST important is for the medical social worker to

    A. establish a sound social diagnosis
    B. outline the functions of her agency
    C. be aware of treatment possibilities
    D. listen closely and plan treatment
    E. determine what the client sees as the problem

5. The one of the following which is the PRIMARY function of a medical social consultant in a family welfare agency is to

    A. carry a case load of families having medical problems
    B. interpret the medical diagnoses to the clients
    C. confer directly with doctors concerning the clients' medical needs
    D. study the health needs of the families
    E. assist the case workers in the handling of medical problems

6. The one of the following which is the PRIMARY function of the family welfare agency is to

   A. provide convalescent care for sick children
   B. establish need and eligibility for proper housing for low income families in order to meet minimum health standards
   C. supervise family relations, thereby insuring the welfare and prevention of delinquency of children
   D. offer vocational rehabilitation services and encourage employment of the handicapped person
   E. help individuals and families meet problems and make the best possible adjustment within their limitations

7. The one of the following social workers who is well–known for her work in social diagnosis is

   A. Bertha Reynolds   B. Janet Thornton
   C. Antoinette Cannon   D. Harriet Bartlett
   E. Mabel McGuire

8. The one of the following which is the PRIMARY function of the social service exchange is to

   A. distinguish the frauds from the needy cases in almsgiving
   B. promote more efficient service to individuals
   C. discourage professional begging through the recording system
   D. insure a fair distribution of welfare funds to agencies
   E. distinguish worthy from unworthy families prior to giving assistance

9. The one of the following which is NOT considered a function of the private family agency is the

   A. rehabilitation of the handicapped through *sheltered employment*
   B. planning of summer camp placements for underprivileged children
   C. assisting of unwed mothers in planning for adoption of their babies
   D. giving of consultant and referral service for the indigent
   E. giving of supplemental financial assistance to marginal income families

10. The author of SOCIAL WORK RECORDING is

    A. Grace White   B. Bertha Reynolds
    C. Gordon Hamilton   D. Richard Cabot
    E. Carol Cooley

11. The one of the following functions which should NEVER be assumed by a medical social worker in a hospital is

    A. planning convalescent care for private patients
    B. routine social review for certain groups
    C. accepting surrenders of babies for adoption
    D. social admitting of indigent patients
    E. terminal care planning, if necessary

12. The one of the following which is the PRIMARY responsibility of any hospital is to   12._____

    A. keep adequate records on all patients
    B. train the medical staff adequately
    C. assist in the advancement of medical knowledge
    D. render care to the sick and injured
    E. promote community health and wellbeing

13. As the medical social worker in a hospital, you have submitted the necessary forms to   13._____
    the Department of Social Services for a prenatal patient to be granted elastic stockings
    because of severe varicosities. After four weeks have elapsed, the patient reports that
    she has not received the stockings.
    The one of the following procedures which you should follow is to

    A. call the social investigator on the case
    B. notify the investigato's supervisor
    C. tell the patient that such matters take a long time
    D. purchase stockings through hospital funds
    E. call the appropriate medical social worker at the Department of Social Services

14. The one of the following which is the PRIMARY function of the social case work supervi-   14._____
    sor in a hospital setting is to

    A. act as a liaison between the administration and the workers
    B. assist and teach her workers to do their job adequately
    C. teach workers, doctors, and nurses the value of case work
    D. administer the expenditures of funds
    E. determine policies of the department as they affect the hospital

15. Assume that as the medical social worker in a hospital, you are called to the accident   15._____
    ward. The doctor states that the unconscious woman on the table has had a miscarriage
    and it will be necessary to admit her for a curettage. Her four children, age 6, 4, 3, and 2,
    are in the waiting room of the hospital. Police report that there are no relatives at the
    address given.
    The one of the following which should be your FIRST step in the case is to

    A. clear the case with social service exchange
    B. call the child care division of the Department of Social Services
    C. arrange for homemaker service
    D. place the children in an emergency shelter
    E. take the children to the Speedwell Society

16. A patient in a voluntary hospital dispensary is in need of a regular supply of bandages and sterile dressings because of a diagnosis of incurable cancer. The patient's family who has been supporting him is unable to meet this additional expense.
The one of the following which would be the BEST procedure for the medical social worker in the hospital to follow is to

    A. send the patient to a city hospital which by law must provide dressings
    B. obtain the necessary form from the Department of Social Services to authorize the hospital pharmacy to dispense these articles
    C. advise the patient to make bandages and sterile dressings
    D. send an order in duplicate for these to the Department of Social Services
    E. contact the local chapter of the American Cancer Society

17. Suppose that a patient in a voluntary hospital is to be transferred to a nursing home in another borough of the city. She has no funds to pay for transportation by an ambulance. Of the following, transfer by ambulance should be arranged through the

    A. Department of Hospitals
    B. Social Service Department of a private hospital
    C. Department of Health
    D. Department of Social Services
    E. Shut-In Society

18. The one of the following statements which is TRUE in regard to the voluntary, non-profit hospitals is that

    A. they are exempt from paying taxes
    B. patients must subject themselves for research purposes
    C. payments may be made only for the exact cost of medical care
    D. the Department of Health has no control over them
    E. no doctor may receive compensation for services rendered

19. Of the following, the CHIEF value of the medical social worker's attendance at ward rounds and conferences with the doctors on service is that

    A. knowledge of medical matters gives security to the worker
    B. the social and medical planning can be coordinated
    C. the worker can report verbally to the doctor rather than dictate extensive records
    D. the patient sees the worker as a part of the medical team
    E. the doctors find it convenient to make referrals at that time

20. The one of the following to whom the director of the social service department of a voluntary hospital is generally responsible is the

    A. United Hospital Fund
    B. board of managers
    C. director of nurses
    D. hospital administrator
    E. medical advisory committee

21. Volunteers can be an asset in the functioning of any hospital. 21.____
The one of the following which represents their GREATEST value to the hospital from the point of view of public relations is

    A. interpreting the hospital to the community
    B. popularizing the hospital with the patients by meeting their personal needs
    C. replacing employees during the labor shortage
    D. lowering the cost of caring for the sick
    E. giving service to visiting relatives which might not otherwise be available

22. The one of the following hospitals which is operated by the Department of Hospitals is 22.____

    A. the Hospital for Joint Diseases
    B. Columbus Hospital
    C. Gouverneur Hospital
    D. Brooklyn Thoracic Hospital
    E. Montefiore Hospital

23. Assume that you are the medical social worker in a clinic. A patient complains to you 23.____
about the time involved in clinic attendance, questioning particularly the need for repeated clinic visits prior to his being given treatment recommendations.
The one of the following you should do FIRST is to

    A. explain that the doctors give their time free, and patience is necessary
    B. interpret the needs of each patient who is waiting at the clinic at the time
    C. describe the overcrowding and the need for better community resources
    D. interpret the possible necessity of laboratory procedures prior to accurate diagnosis and treatment measures
    E. discuss the length of time involved in visiting a private doctor during his office hours

24. If a forty-year-old woman with severe rheumatic heart disease requests her doctor to 24.____
sterilize her by a tubal ligation, he may do so legally PROVIDED he

    A. can testify that further pregnancies would be dangerous
    B. has the consent of the woman with two witnesses present
    C. has the signed consent of the woman and her husband
    D. explains the nature of the operation to the woman and her husband
    E. has a court order to perform the operation

25. In regard to the care of the chronically ill, the one of the following which is recommended 25.____
CHIEFLY is the

    A. establishment of more chronic hospitals specifically designated as caring only for the chronically ill
    B. establishment of more hospital facilities for their care in the community general hospitals
    C. placing of greater responsibility for their care upon relatives and friends
    D. payment of larger fees to the privately owned nursing homes
    E. conduct of research into the causes of chronic illness by a greater number of voluntary hospitals

KEY (CORRECT ANSWERS)

1.	E	11.	C
2.	B	12.	D
3.	D	13.	E
4.	E	14.	B
5.	E	15.	B
6.	E	16.	E
7.	A	17.	A
8.	B	18.	A
9.	E	19.	B
10.	C	20.	D

21. A
22. C
23. D
24. C
25. B

TEST 2

DIRECTIONS: Each question or incomplete statement is followed by several suggested answers or completions. Select the one that BEST answers the question or completes the statement. *PRINT THE LETTER OF THE CORRECT ANSWER IN THE SPACE AT THE RIGHT.*

1. It is important for a medical social worker to have a basic knowledge of medical information MAINLY because

   A. in working with the doctor she must prove her competence
   B. patients will ask pertinent questions regarding diagnosis and treatment of their illnesses
   C. she can encourage patients to maintain good health standards
   D. the social problems of the patients may vary according to the nature of their illnesses
   E. she can help patients to avoid the major illnesses

   1.____

2. In order to be admitted to a state tuberculosis sanitarium, the patient MUST

   A. be diagnosed as an active tuberculosis case
   B. be unable to pay for private care
   C. have legal residence in the state
   D. apply for admission through the division of handicapped
   E. commit himself

   2.____

3. The one of the following which is the PRIMARY aim of public health programs in relation to illness and disease is to

   A. cure
   B. palliate
   C. prevent
   D. conduct research
   E. ameliorate

   3.____

4. Every child before admission to school is required to be vaccinated against

   A. smallpox
   B. diphtheria
   C. typhoid
   D. scarlet fever
   E. whooping cough

   4.____

5. Cancer is considered a public health responsibility MAINLY because of the

   A. enormity of the problem
   B. lack of adequate diagnostic facilities
   C. need for research
   D. familial disposition
   E. value of contact examination

   5.____

6. The one of the following whom the U.S. Children's Bureau would NOT consider a crippled or a handicapped child is a child with

   A. cerebral palsy
   B. nephrosis
   C. poliomyelitis
   D. a cardiac disorder
   E. a club foot

   6.____

7. The one of the following which is the PRIMARY function of the American Heart Association is

   A. fundraising for indigent patients
   B. promotion of research
   C. provision of convalescent facilities
   D. education of the public
   E. supervision of heart clinics

8. The one of the following which is NOT a function of the visiting nurse organizations is

   A. relief of the sick in their homes
   B. giving injections to patients at home
   C. supervising health care of the newborn at home
   D. education of the patient group to give adequate care to the patient
   E. full-time bedside nursing care in the home

9. The father of a man in the armed forces became seriously ill and was hospitalized in a critical condition. He kept calling for his son, who was stationed in this country. The one of the following you would call in order to ask that the son be granted a leave to see his father is the

   A. American Legion   B. son's commanding officer
   C. Veterans Administration D. Traveler's Aid Society
   E. American Red Cross

10. The one of the following which is a convalescent home for the care of cardiac patients with rheumatic fever is

    A. Elizabeth House   B. Eleanora's Home
    C. Francis Sanatorium   D. Charles Hospital
    E. Giles' Home

11. The one of the following which BEST describes the Welfare Council is:

    A. A council of agencies to decide upon the functioning of each member agency
    B. A group of lay persons whose function is to insure good welfare practices
    C. A council of wealthy citizens, with one paid employee, to give informational service
    D. A council of social agencies to coordinate existing welfare services
    E. The central channel for the collection and distribution of welfare funds

12. The one of the following agencies which is NOT a settlement house is the

    A. Hudson Guild   B. House of St. Giles
    C. Casita Maria   D. Greenwich House
    E. Hartley House

13. The one of the following circumstances which will warrant a *home teacher* for a child reg- 13._____
    istered in a grammar school is if

    A. he is registered in a public school
    B. he will be unable to attend regular school for at least a month
    C. he has been known to suffer from a lack of schooling
    D. his family is agreeable to the plan and will cooperate
    E. his intelligence quotient demonstrates he will benefit by this

14. In order to have a child admitted to the Willowbrook Hospital, application must be made 14._____
    to the

    A. City Department of Hospitals
    B. City Department of Health
    C. State Department of Mental Hygiene
    D. State Board of Social Services
    E. City Department of Correction

15. There are no private or voluntary hospitals in the city whose PRIMARY function is the 15._____
    treatment of

    A. orthopedic diseases   B. the chronically ill
    C. cancer   D. nervous diseases
    E. contagious diseases

16. Of the following, those who are legally entitled to special preference when applying for 16._____
    housing through the Housing Authority are

    A. handicapped persons
    B. persons in the lowest income group
    C. persons in rooming houses
    D. honorably discharged veterans
    E. families with many children

17. The one of the following which is the PRIMARY purpose of the Worker's Compensa- 17._____
    tion Law is to

    A. protect both the employer and the employee
    B. insure full pay to sick workers
    C. insure favorable work conditions in dangerous positions
    D. eliminate *sweat shop labor* and maintain adequate wages
    E. replace the need for unions in large factories

18. A person whose employment comes within the provisions of the State Unemployment 18._____
    Compensation Act, upon losing his position, is ALWAYS entitled to receive unemploy-
    ment compensation if he

    A. is unable to obtain work in his specialized field
    B. applies for compensation within 48 hours of the termination of his employment
    C. has worked in certain occupations for a specific number of quarters in the previous
       year
    D. is able to prove that he lost his employment through no fault of his own
    E. can prove that his family will be in need until he obtains employment again

19. A legally married woman who has been living continuously with her husband bears a child who she claims is not her husband's child.
The one of the following statements which is TRUE in connection with the placing of this child for legal adoption is that the

   A. alleged father must give his consent for adoption
   B. mother alone is required to give her consent for adoption
   C. child cannot be adopted legally
   D. alleged father must prove the child was his
   E. woman's husband must give his consent for adoption

19.___

20. Many states have passed the so-called disability benefit laws.
The one of the following which is a TRUE statement in connection with these laws is that

   A. cash benefits for occupational injuries or illnesses are paid
   B. the employer must pay all employees half salary when illness occurs
   C. both employees and employers are covered by insurance to meet the cost of their illness
   D. cash benefits are paid to workers who lose wages because of non-occupational illness or accident
   E. the federal government will pay administrative costs of enforcement

20.___

KEY (CORRECT ANSWERS)

1.	D	11.	D
2.	A	12.	B
3.	C	13.	B
4.	A	14.	C
5.	A	15.	E
6.	B	16.	D
7.	D	17.	A
8.	E	18.	C
9.	E	19.	E
10.	C	20.	D

TEST 3

DIRECTIONS: Each question or incomplete statement is followed by several suggested answers or completions. Select the one that BEST answers the question or completes the statement. *PRINT THE LETTER OF THE CORRECT ANSWER IN THE SPACE AT THE RIGHT.*

1. The one of the following which is a TRUE statement about the Social Security Act is that it   1.____

    A. provides with a pension everyone who is over 65 years old
    B. ensures financial security for children of aged parents
    C. provides a minimum economic basic security for millions
    D. eliminates poverty under our present economy
    E. provides employment for the older age group

2. The one of the following which was MOST recently added to the categories of federal public assistance is   2.____

    A. aid to the permanently disabled
    B. aid to dependent children
    C. aid to the blind
    D. old age assistance
    E. home relief

3. Of the following statements relating to social security, the one which is TRUE is that   3.____

    A. a person receiving a monthly social security check may receive supplementary assistance from the Department of Social Services
    B. every person over 65 years of age is entitled to benefits through the Bureau of Old Age and Survivors' Insurance
    C. a person must give positive proof that he is in need and has no relatives to assist him before he is eligible for a social security check
    D. a person who lives in an old age home is not eligible to receive a social security check
    E. a person may receive a social security check while he is working provided he does not earn over $5,000 a year

4. Under the social security laws, a mother with children under 16 years may ALWAYS obtain an Aid to Dependent Children allotment if   4.____

    A. her husband is killed in the line of duty in the United States Armed Services
    B. she proves that, due to her husband's illness or death, the family is in financial need
    C. she is widowed and is unable to obtain gainful employment
    D. she has demonstrated that it is necessary for her to remain at home with her children
    E. the husband has deserted the family

57

5. The one of the following programs which is administered and operated ONLY by the federal government is

   A. services for crippled children
   B. aid to the needy blind
   C. aid to dependent children
   D. old age and survivors' insurance
   E. aid to the permanently disabled

6. Under the Department of Health, Education, and Welfare, there is provision for a federal-state program of vocational rehabilitation.
   The one of the following which is the BASIC objective of the total program is to

   A. prevent disabling diseases
   B. restore disabled persons in body and spirit
   C. provide appliances where necessary
   D. rehabilitate the mentally defective
   E. retrain disabled servicemen

7. The one of the following agencies which administers the U.S. Public Health Service is the

   A. U.S. Children's Bureau
   B. Treasury Department
   C. National Security Resources Board
   D. National Research Council
   E. Department of Health, Education and Welfare

8. The one of the following which historically was the FIRST function of what is now the U.S. Public Health Service is

   A. the provision of medical and hospital care for the nation's merchant seamen
   B. research into the causes of contagious diseases
   C. the establishment of the Pure Food and Drug Act
   D. the provision of care for the mentally disturbed
   E. administration of city and state departments of health

9. The one of the following U.S. Public Health Service hospitals which gives treatment to narcotic addicts is the

   A. Freedmen's Hospital, Washington, D.C.
   B. Carville Hospital, Carville, La.
   C. U.S. Public Health Service Hospital, Lexington, Ky.
   D. U.S. Public Health Service Hospital, Stapleton, S.I., N.Y.
   E. U.S. Public Health Service Hospital, Manhattan Beach, Brooklyn, N.Y.

Questions 10-15.

DIRECTIONS: Questions 10 through 15 are to be answered SOLELY on the basis of the facts given below.

CASE A

A forty-eight-year old single woman who has Parkinson's syndrome comes to the dispensary of a voluntary general hospital for treatment of excessive vaginal bleeding. She is admitted to the hospital as a *City case* after she proves that she is supported by a Department of Social Services allowance. She has been living in a furnished room and has been receiving a restaurant allowance. A biopsy is done, and a diagnosis of advanced carcinoma of the cervix is made. The hospital is not equipped to treat the patient and wishes her transferred to a city hospital for surgery.

10. As a *City case,* the one of the following statements which is TRUE is that

    A. only emergency treatment pending transfer to the city hospital will be rendered
    B. the city will assume the complete cost of any medical care rendered
    C. the patient's welfare checks will be used to pay her hospital expenses
    D. the voluntary hospital will be reimbursed by the city for care given on a per diem basis
    E. as a non-paying patient, she agrees to enter the voluntary hospital for diagnostic and research purposes only

11. Of the following, the BEST definition of biopsy is

    A. an examination of the substance obtained through a gastric lavage
    B. the removal and microscopic examination of a piece of tissue
    C. a laboratory examination of vaginal bleeding
    D. a blood test showing cancer cells in the bloodstream
    E. a fluoroscopic examination of a body organ

12. The one of the following departments which may authorize the transfer of this patient from the voluntary to the city hospital is the

    A. Department of Social Services
    B. Police Department
    C. Department of Health
    D. Department of Hospitals
    E. Department of Investigation

13. If, as the medical social worker in the voluntary hospital, you have known this woman and have been aware of her fear of surgery, the one of the following steps which would be BEST for you to take in order to help her in this transfer to a city hospital is to

    A. tell her that you will call the medical social worker in the city hospital who will help her during her stay there
    B. tell her that you will discuss her fears with the doctor at the city hospital
    C. promise to visit her at the city hospital and keep in touch with her
    D. tell her that the Department of Social Services investigator will visit her at the city hospital
    E. describe to her all the things which will be done during the surgery to allay her fears

14. When the Department of Social Services investigator hears of the patient's illness and hospitalization, the one of the following actions which he should take IMMEDIATELY is to

   A. close the case pending diagnosis
   B. notify the landlord not to hold the room
   C. recall any checks issued within the past ten days
   D. visit the patient in the hospital
   E. telephone the hospital for verification

15. Suppose the patient is to be discharged from the city hospital following surgery, but will need two or three months of nursing home care before she is able to return to living alone in a furnished room.
   The one of the following which will have to finance such nursing home care is the

   A. American Cancer Society
   B. Department of Social Services
   C. Ladies' Auxiliary of the city hospital
   D. patient's relatives or friends
   E. Department of Hospitals

Questions 16-17.

DIRECTIONS: Questions 16 and 17 are to be answered SOLELY on the basis of the facts given below.

CASE B

A 22-year-old pregnant woman was referred to medical social service by the nurse in the clinic of a city hospital. The nurse reported that the patient had cried following the examination which disclosed her pregnancy and, when questioned by the doctor, she said she was very distressed by her marital situation. You, as the medical social worker assigned to the case, learn that her husband is the superintendent of the house in which they live and that he receives free rent but no salary. He does odd jobs to earn money and buys groceries and other necessities, but will not give his wife any money. The husband drinks very heavily.

The patient says this is her second pregnancy. The first child, now 15 months old, was born five months after her marriage. She says she wants to leave her husband but wonders how she can support her babies. She would agree to stay with her husband if he would give her money.

16. On the basis of the facts given in Case B, the one of the following steps you would take is:

   A. Referral to the Department of Social Services
   B. Referral to a family agency
   C. Referral to Domestic Relations Court
   D. Discussion of the problem with the patient's husband
   E. Discussion of the problem with available relatives

17. As the patient described in Case B has no relatives, she is also concerned as to who will take care of her 15-month-old daughter during her confinement.
The one of the following suggestions which would be MOST helpful is that

   A. application be made to the child care division of the Department of Social Services
   B. her husband take over this responsibility
   C. a neighbor take the child into her home
   D. the child be taken to the Children's Shelter
   E. application be made to a family agency for homemaker service

17._____

Questions 18-20.

DIRECTIONS: Questions 18 through 20 are to be answered SOLELY on the basis of the facts given below.

CASE C

A woman, pregnant out of wedlock, in her 8th month of pregnancy, cones to you as the medical social worker in a city hospital, asking you to arrange for the adoption of her baby. She says she has no friends and is not interested in any plan for the baby other than adoption.

18. The one of the following agencies to which you would refer the woman described in Case C is the

   A. Spence-Chapin Adoption Service
   B. Bureau of Child Welfare of the Department of Social Services
   C. Surrogates' Court
   D. Domestic Relations Court
   E. Aid to Dependent Children Division of the Department of Social Services

18._____

19. The woman described in Case C is presently living in a furnished room and cannot pay the coming week's rent. She is Catholic and is willing to enter a shelter for unmarried mothers.
The one of the following shelters to which you would seek admission for her is

   A. The Wm. Booth Memorial Home and Hospital
   B. Inwood House
   C. The Heartsease Home for Women and Babies
   D. St. Faith's House
   E. The Guild of the Infant Saviour

19._____

20. When the baby is ready for adoption, the one of the following courts which would have jurisdiction over the adoption proceedings is the _____ Court.

   A. Criminal
   B. Surrogates'
   C. Family Division of Domestic Relations
   D. County
   E. Children's Court of Domestic Relations

20._____

KEY (CORRECT ANSWERS)

1. C
2. A
3. A
4. B
5. D

6. B
7. E
8. A
9. C
10. D

11. B
12. D
13. A
14. E
15. B

16. B
17. A
18. B
19. E
20. B

EXAMINATION SECTION
TEST 1

DIRECTIONS: Each question or incomplete statement is followed by several suggested answers or completions. Select the one that BEST answers the question or completes the statement. *PRINT THE LETTER OF THE CORRECT ANSWER IN THE SPACE AT THE RIGHT.*

1. The one of the following which is the BEST reason for a medical social worker's having a sound foundation of medical information is that she may be able to

    A. determine the degree of disability which each illness may cause
    B. assist the doctors in bringing about solutions to medical problems
    C. instruct visiting nurses in case work
    D. instruct patients in the proper way to carry out medical recommendations
    E. work intelligently as a member of the medical team in helping sick people make the best use of medical care

1.____

2. The one of the following which a medical social worker should consider the LEAST desirable during the course of the treatment interview with the client is to

    A. foster a totally dependent attitude
    B. respect the client's judgment
    C. permit the client to talk about possible solutions
    D. respect the client as an individual person
    E. clear the air and let the client talk

2.____

3. The one of the following which is MOST likely to be the medical social worker's role with a clinic patient who has a mild case of diabetes is to

    A. help the patient change his environment
    B. help the patient accept his illness
    C. arrange for the placement of his children
    D. arrange for blood sugar tests
    E. arrange convalescent care

3.____

4. The one of the following which is the PRIMARY purpose of the teaching of medical students by a medical social worker is to

    A. impress upon them the responsibilities of the medical social worker
    B. increase the number of referrals to the medical social worker
    C. make them aware of the social and emotional factors which may complicate the care of patients
    D. describe the development of social work to them
    E. teach them medical social casework

4.____

5. The one of the following functions which is agreed by medical social work authorities to be the PROPER focus of a modern medical social service department is

    A. teaching social aspects of medicine
    B. assisting in research
    C. providing medical relief
    D. completing brief service cases
    E. performing casework

5.____

63

6. Medical social work authorities consider a 100% review of a diagnostic group in a hospital an appropriate activity of a medical social worker under certain circumstances PROVIDED the purpose is

   A. individualization
   B. health education
   C. transference
   D. steering
   E. medical follow-up

7. In addition to basic knowledge of social work, the one of the following in which medical social workers are expected to have SPECIAL ability is

   A. recognizing the symptoms of early illness
   B. first aid
   C. follow-up of tuberculosis contacts
   D. working in a team-work relationship with other professions in a medical agency
   E. planning recreation programs in hospital wards

8. The administrator of a hospital is responsible for the total functioning of the institution, and each department head is responsible to the administrator for the proper functioning of his department. Assuming that you are a medical social worker in the hospital and a student nurse is extremely insolent to you or to a patient in your presence, the one of the following to whom you should report her action is

   A. the doctor on service
   B. the director of nurses
   C. your immediate supervisor
   D. the registered nurse on the floor
   E. the hospital administrator

9. An acutely ill mother of a healthy two-week old infant girl is admitted to a hospital at night. The following morning, the husband of the patient phones the medical social worker on the service and demands to know why the baby was refused readmission to the hospital nursery when it only left there the week before.
   The one of the following replies which the medical social worker SHOULD give to the husband is that

   A. there are no vacant bassinets in the nursery
   B. the baby was not admitted to the nursery because she is not sick
   C. if social service had been on duty, the baby would have been admitted
   D. he should report the matter to the medical superintendent
   E. infants are never admitted to the nursery from outside the hospital

10. The one of the following which is the PRIMARY role of social casework is to

    A. direct people who have little knowledge of life toward more satisfying experiences
    B. readjust environmental factors which are hindering a person's social adjustment
    C. help people recognize and handle problems which are not beyond their capacity to solve
    D. give sympathetic understanding to individuals who have social problems
    E. refer individuals to the proper community resource to meet their needs

11. The one of the following which is the PRIME requisite of a good social worker is a   11.____

    A. respect for the worth of an individual
    B. high degree of intelligence
    C. knowledge of psychiatry and mental hygiene
    D. sound knowledge of resources
    E. good knowledge of human behavior

12. Of the following, the one which is the BEST definition of social casework is   12.____

    A. a substitute for proper family relations
    B. a treatment process for sick persons
    C. a method of mass treatment of social problems
    D. an individual approach to people in trouble
    E. a method of solving financial problems

13. The one of the following which may be said to have come FIRST in the history and development of social work as a profession is   13.____

    A. analytical assistance
    B. friendly visiting by volunteer workers
    C. psychological approach
    D. outdoor relief
    E. social diagnoses

14. The one of the following circumstances in which casework service would be MOST likely to bring about a *successful* solution is in a situation in which   14.____

    A. a family is satisfied with things as they are
    B. the attitudes and habits of a patient are firmly entrenched and of long standing
    C. for one reason or another, there is only financial need
    D. the worker is working for the community against the desires of the patient
    E. a family seeks help with the problem of an adolescent child

15. The one of the following which is an IDEAL social casework situation is a(n)   15.____

    A. prisoner released from a reformatory who is very penitent for his crime
    B. person who is pronounced cured of congenital syphilis
    C. unwed mother who is seeking assistance by court action to punish the putative father
    D. psychoneurotic patient who is aware that her problems come from within her environment and her reaction to this environment
    E. person who knows he needs help, is capable of cooperating, and seeks some solution to his problem

16. In distinguishing between functions of a public agency and a private agency, the one of the following functions which would MOST likely belong only to a private agency is to   16.____

    A. investigate occupational resources
    B. investigate need for complete financial assistance
    C. evaluate need of an individual for rehabilitation
    D. do casework with the marginal income group
    E. determine budgetary needs of the indigent group

17. The one of the following services to patients which is not considered as legitimately falling within the functions of the medical social service department of a hospital is the

   A. securing of appliances
   B. arranging for convalescent care
   C. arranging for day care for children
   D. dispensing of medications
   E. reporting to community agencies

18. A voluntary hospital is a hospital

   A. in which doctors are forbidden to accept fees
   B. which accepts only patients unable to pay the full cost of their care
   C. which is entirely supported by public contributions
   D. in which most of the hospital workers are volunteers
   E. which is a non-profit institution

19. The one of the following which is a TRUE statement regarding the commissioner of hospitals is that he is

   A. responsible for the health of all residents of the city
   B. appointed by the mayor
   C. required to sign all commitment papers
   D. responsible only to the governor of the state
   E. an elected official for a two-year term

20. The one of the following which is a TRUE statement is that medical care in a tax-supported hospital is available to

   A. only those who have settlement in the area
   B. only those receiving public assistance
   C. all persons in need of medical treatment
   D. emergency cases only
   E. persons with contagious diseases only

21. The one of the following which is the PRIMARY function of the department of health is

   A. the treatment of contagious diseases
   B. education of the public towards better health
   C. conducting statistical research in problems of health
   D. providing nursing service to the indigent
   E. the distribution of health literature

22. A premarital blood test is required prior to the issuance of a marriage license. This requirement may be waived when

   A. both parties have been married before to different spouses
   B. the woman is pregnant at the time the marriage license is requested
   C. both parties have had physical examinations by a private physician
   D. both parties present reports of negative blood tests taken 6 months prior to the request for a license
   E. the man is over 65 years of age and in apparent good health

23. The one of the following statements regarding the care and treatment of tuberculous patients in the state which is FALSE is:

    A. If it is established that an alien was suffering from tuberculosis at the time of landing or becomes a public charge as a result of this condition within five years, he is eligible for sanitarium care for a one-year period in a federal hospital
    B. Any person affected with a communicable disease such as tuberculosis, likely to be dangerous to the lives and health of other persons, may be removed to a hospital designated by a board of health, upon the report of a duly authorized physician
    C. Care and treatment provided by the state or by any county or city for persons suffering from tuberculosis shall be available without cost or charge to any person having state residence and at the discretion of the state commissioner of health to any other person in the state who is suffering from tuberculosis
    D. Persons approved for admission to state hospitals unable to pay for transportation may be furnished such transportation by the superintendent of the hospital, and that transportation to another hospital for special care and treatment may also be furnished
    E. Any person who volunteers to assume and pay for the cost of the care and treatment of a patient suffering from tuberculosis shall be permitted to do so, but no state, county, city, or other public official shall request or require such payment

24. The one of the following which forms a PRIMARY aim of school child guidance clinics is the

    A. treatment of the parents
    B. prevention of juvenile delinquency
    C. prevention of mental ill health
    D. prevention of truancy
    E. treatment of the narcotic addict

25. The Community Chest and the Council of Social Agencies in cities where both exist work cooperatively to provide the greatest welfare for the entire community. The one of the following functions which would fall EXCLUSIVELY within the functions of the Community Chest is to

    A. give group work service to the community
    B. provide recreational facilities to members
    C. support agency functions and programs
    D. raise funds for the social welfare and health agencies
    E. interpret the work of individual agencies

26. The one of the following which is the PRIMARY function of the Tuberculosis and Health Association is

    A. psychometric testing
    B. convalescent care
    C. education of the public
    D. financial assistance
    E. surgical treatment

27. The one of the following which is the CHIEF purpose of the visits paid by a public health nurse to a patient in his home is to

   A. educate patient or patient group to give adequate care
   B. make epidemiological investigations
   C. report to the truant authority
   D. give reassurance to patient and patient group
   E. evaluate the home situation for emotional and physical strains

28. When a post-partum patient and her baby are discharged after a week in a hospital and the case is referred to the Visiting Nurse Service, the one of the following which is the USUAL routine for the visiting nurse is to

   A. visit daily for the next week to check on the mother's condition and to bathe the baby
   B. arrange for housekeeping service if it seems necessary
   C. keep in touch with the nurse in the school attended by other children in the family to avoid exposing the baby to a communicable disease
   D. keep the referral on file unless the patient is under a physician's care at home
   E. visit within a short time of the patient's return home to instruct her in the care of the baby

29. A 35-year-old woman who had always lived in New York City was diagnosed as having osteomyelitis of the left tibia, and was admitted to a New York City hospital for treatment. Conservative treatment was of no avail, and she had an amputation below the left knee. The medical social worker was called in to see her as she said she had spent five months in San Francisco, California, just prior to her hospitalization and had no means of support. She needed an artificial leg before leaving the hospital, plus financial support. Before her illness, she was a typist.
   The one of the following agencies which should be contacted FIRST is the

   A. New York State Department of Social Services
   B. California State Department of Welfare
   C. New York State Division of Vocational Rehabilitation
   D. Welfare Council of New York City
   E. Rehabilitation Division of the New York City Department of Hospitals

30. When the woman described in the preceding question was ready to leave the hospital and the medical social worker was seeking financial support for maintenance, the one of the following agencies which SHOULD be contacted is the

   A. Department of Social Services
   B. Florence Crittenton League
   C. Division of Placement and Unemployment Insurance
   D. Workmen's Compensation Office
   E. Community Service Society

7(#1)

31. The name of the following institutions which is NOT under the management and control of the State Department of Correction is the   31.____

    A. Berkshire Industrial Farm
    B. Wallkill Prison
    C. Woodbourne Correctional Institution
    D. Elmira Reformatory
    E. State Vocational Institution

32. The one of the following which can be considered the PRIMARY purpose of the Social Security Act is the   32.____

    A. insurance against loss of earnings by an injured employee
    B. furthering of the security of the citizen and his family through social insurance
    C. distribution of surplus wealth among the needy classes
    D. development of an economic balance between the wealthy and the poor
    E. insurance of dependents against need

33. The passage of the Social Security Act in 1935 points toward the establishment of a broad national welfare program. The one of the following ways in which federal funds are provided, according to the provisions of the Act, is through   33.____

    A. payment of all the administrative funds used in disbursing state and local funds
    B. maintenance of adequate institutions to foster a good national program
    C. lump sum payments to all needy blind and widows
    D. part payment in participation with state and local funds
    E. full payment to individual recipients

34. The one of the following groups of persons which is ELIGIBLE for benefits under the Social Security Act is   34.____

    A. persons who have worked a required period of time in certain covered occupations
    B. the dependents of workmen injured or killed while on the job
    C. all those over 65 years old who are unable to find employment
    D. the dependents of soldiers, sailors, or marines killed while on combat duty
    E. all citizens who have reached the age of 65 years, whether or not in need of financial assistance

35. Of the following categories, the one which was MOST recently added to those which are covered under the Social Security Act is   35.____

    A. the blind
    B. the permanently disabled
    C. crippled adults
    D. the aged
    E. dependent children

KEY (CORRECT ANSWERS)

1. E	11. A	21. B	31. A
2. A	12. D	22. B	32. B
3. B	13. B	23. A	33. D
4. C	14. E	24. C	34. A
5. E	15. E	25. D	35. B
6. A	16. D	26. C	
7. D	17. D	27. A	
8. C	18. E	28. E	
9. E	19. B	29. C	
10. C	20. C	30. A	

EXAMINATION SECTION
TEST 1

DIRECTIONS: Each question or incomplete statement is followed by several suggested answers or completions. Select the one that BEST answers the question or completes the statement. *PRINT THE LETTER OF THE CORRECT ANSWER IN THE SPACE AT THE RIGHT.*

1. Of the following, the MOST important reason for requiring that an employee have knowledge of medical office procedures is that

    A. she can take care of sick people in the absence of a doctor
    B. patients in the clinic will be impressed with her apparent knowledge
    C. she will be more helpful in her work at the clinic
    D. letters she may have to write will be more concise

2. A newly appointed employee should have a good understanding of her functions in the Department of Health.
Of the following, the training which would be LEAST helpful to her in the performance of her functions is

    A. an understanding of the role of the Department of Health in the community
    B. development of skill in the technics of work in a health center
    C. information as to the services offered in the health center
    D. development of skill in the care of the sick in their own homes

3. If an employee were called upon at the same time to attend to each of the following, the one she should do FIRST is

    A. sterilize instruments used in the examination of the last patient
    B. answer the telephone
    C. give the patient who is just leaving another appointment
    D. check to see if a patient who has just arrived has an appointment

4. Of the following, the LEAST important reason for answering telephone calls promptly in the health clinic is that

    A. patients waiting in the clinic will be impressed with the self-importance of the employee
    B. patients calling for information will be answered quickly
    C. the public will get a favorable impression of the Department of Health
    D. it will result in better service by keeping the lines free for other calls

5. Assume that the physician assigned to the clinic in which you work calls the clinic and tells you that he has been detained for half an hour and will not be able to report at 1:00 P.M. as scheduled.
You should

    A. not say anything about the call to anyone
    B. report this information to your immediate supervisor
    C. tell the patient scheduled for 1:00 P.M. to come back the next day
    D. tell the physician that he must come at 1:00 P.M. since a patient has been scheduled for that time

6. Assume that a physician who is examining a patient asks you to hand him a certain instrument from the tray. You do not know exactly what he is referring to.
The BEST thing for you to do is to

   A. give him an instrument which you think might be suitable for the examination
   B. ask him to repeat what he said
   C. admit that you cannot identify the instrument he wants
   D. tell him that there is no such instrument on the tray

7. Assume that a patient asks you to explain something the doctor told her about her illness which she says she does not understand.
For you to suggest that she tell the doctor that she did not understand what he told her and ask him to explain it again is

   A. *advisable;* the patient will be impressed by your interest in her
   B. *inadvisable;* patients get tired of the run-around
   C. *advisable;* the doctor is best qualified to answer questions concerning or affecting the patient's health
   D. *inadvisable;* the patient will lose confidence in your ability

8. Assume that, after you have been employed for several months, the nurse who is your immediate supervisor summons you to her office. She tells you that she has noticed on several occasions that you have been careless about your personal appearance. In this instance, it would be

   A. proper for you to tell her that your personal appearance is no concern of hers
   B. advisable for you to listen politely to her and then do nothing about it
   C. fitting for you to tell her that the other employees in the clinic are just as careless
   D. best for you to thank her for her interest and to tell her that you will make an effort to be more careful

9. One of the patients at the Health Center insists that she be sent to a different doctor as she does not like the doctor she saw last week.
Of the following answers, the one that is MOST advisable for you to give to the patient is that

   A. she will have to take whatever doctor is available
   B. all the clinic doctors are equally good
   C. you will try to send her to another doctor
   D. she should see the nurse in charge

10. Suppose that the doctor in the clinic has given you an order which is contrary to the usual clinic procedure. Of the following, the BEST action for you to take is to

    A. point out to the doctor the usual clinic procedure and then do as he tells you
    B. refuse to do what he tells you as it is contrary to the usual procedure
    C. refuse to do what he tells you and call the nurse in charge
    D. do as the doctor tells you and at the first opportunity report the occurrence to the nurse in charge

11. When filing some patients' record cards in an alphabetic file, you notice that one card obviously has been misfiled.
    In this case, it would be MOST advisable for you to

    A. pay no attention to this as you believe it was not your error
    B. pull out the card and file it correctly
    C. report this to the clinic supervisor and suggest to her that she reprimand the employee who you believe is responsible for the misfiling
    D. take no particular care in the future when filing cards since errors will occur anyway

11.____

12. Assume that you are working directly with children in a well baby clinic. You feel feverish.
    Of the following, the BEST action for you to take is to

    A. wait and see whether you feel better; you don't want to seem to be a chronic complainer
    B. report immediately to the nurse in charge that you do not feel well
    C. take your temperature and, if it is over 101° F, report to the nurse in charge
    D. report to the nurse in charge only if you have other symptoms

12.____

13. As a receptionist in a public health center, you have certain responsibilities towards patients and other callers. You should greet each caller promptly and courteously. Never keep a caller waiting while you carry on a personal conversation, either on the telephone or with another employee. However, if you are occupied with clinic matters, give the caller to understand that you will be with him in a short while.
    On the basis of this paragraph, if a caller comes in while you are discussing with the nurse in charge coverage of the clinic during the lunch hour, the one of the following actions which would be the BEST for you to take is to

    A. stop and take care of his needs immediately as you should never keep a caller waiting
    B. nod to him and continue making plans for clinic coverage
    C. say to him that you will take care of him in a moment; then finish making your plans for clinic coverage
    D. finish making plans for clinic coverage with the nurse in charge and then inquire into the caller's needs

13.____

14. Assume that you are responsible for scheduling clinic appointments. One of the patients who has to report to the clinic every Tuesday morning asks that his appointments be scheduled for the last half hour of the clinic session. It has been the practice in this clinic to keep the last half hour open only for emergency appointments, and to schedule all appointments in order, from the time when the clinic opens.
    Of the following, the BEST action for you to take is to

    A. schedule the appointment at the time requested by the patient as he probably has a good reason for wanting it then
    B. disregard his request as no one attending a clinic should be given special consideration
    C. deny his request unless he has a medical reason for asking for a late appointment
    D. refer the request to the nurse in charge to determine if he should be given a late appointment

14.____

15. Suppose that a patient who is registered in the Social Hygiene Clinic of a Health Center appears in a drunken condition for a scheduled appointment.
Of the following, the BEST action for you to take is to

    A. inform the nurse in charge of the situation
    B. have him await his turn with the other patients
    C. send him home, telling him not to return until he is sober
    D. arrange for him to see the doctor immediately

16. Assume that you have been asked by your supervisor to instruct a newly-appointed aide in the performance of a given task.
Of the following, the BEST procedure for you to follow is

    A. to check her work only once after you have shown her how to do it; continued supervision after this should be the supervisor's responsibility
    B. not to check her work after you have shown her how to do it as she may resent your supervision
    C. not to check her work immediately but wait until she has done the task several times in order to give her a fair chance
    D. to check her work at frequent intervals after you have shown her how to do it until she is able to perform the given task

17. A worker should be carefully introduced to the clinic to which she has been assigned. The period of orientation will vary widely with the individual, her previous experience, and the type of clinic to which she is assigned.
In general, it will include an introduction to the physical set-up, the personnel, the type of service to be rendered, and the ideals of the clinic. In the beginning, the new worker should be given simple assignments and close supervision. The program should be arranged so as to give the nurse in charge opportunity to study the worker as to personality, general ability, or any special handicaps.
According to this paragraph, the one of the following statements that is MOST accurate is that, during the first few days, the new worker should

    A. do nothing but observe the physical set-up, the personnel, the type of service rendered, the ideals of the clinic
    B. be given a 30 hour course in the clinic to which she is assigned, including the physical set-up, the personnel, the ideals of the clinic
    C. be observed by the nurse in charge as to her ability to do the work in the clinic to which she has been assigned
    D. be closely supervised by the nurse in charge until she has a thorough knowledge of the clinic

18. Preparing a patient for physical examination has important mental aspects. Because each patient is individual in his reactions, a worker must plan her approach so as to deal with these reactions sympathetically. Thus, one patient may be afraid of the pain an examination may cause him immediately, another may fear that he will have unpleasant effects later, and still another may be only curious about the examination and have neither fear nor anxiety.
On the basis of this paragraph, the one of the following statements that BEST describes the reactions of patients when undergoing examination is that all patients

    A. are afraid when being examined
    B. react differently to an examination
    C. are afraid of the after-effects of an examination
    D. are curious about the examination

19. A recently published article states: Weight for height and age is, as many have previously held, an inadequate index of the *nutritional status* of a child. It is unscientific and unfair to set average weight as a goal for all children or for an individual child. Weighing and measuring, however, should be continued as a record of the trend of individual growth which is of value to the physician in relation to other findings and as valuable devices to interest the child in his growth.
According to this article, weighing and measuring the height of children

   A. are of no value and should be stopped
   B. are useful to the physician
   C. are of no value but give interesting information
   D. indicate the nutritional status of the child

20. Blood pressure is the force that the blood exerts against the walls of the vessels through which it flows. The blood pressure is commonly meant to be the pressure in the arteries. The pressure in the arteries varies with the contraction (work period) and the relaxation (rest period) of the heart. When the heart contracts, the blood in the arteries is at its greatest pressure. This is called the systolic pressure. When the heart relaxes, the blood in the arteries is at its lowest pressure. This is called the diastolic pressure. The difference between both pressures is called the pulse pressure.
The one of the following statements that is MOST accurate on the basis of this paragraph is that

   A. the blood in the arteries is at its greatest pressure during contraction
   B. systolic pressure measures the blood in the arteries when the heart is relaxed
   C. blood pressure is determined by obtaining the difference between systolic and diastolic pressure
   D. pulse pressure is the same as blood pressure

21. Lymph is a clear fluid, rich in white blood cells, and is actually blood plasma which has filtered through the walls of capillaries. It is circulated through the lymph vessels and in all the tissue spaces of the body. It carries nourishment and oxygen to the tissues and waste products away from them.
The one of the following statements that is NOT correct on the basis of this paragraph is that lymph

   A. contains red blood cells
   B. contains white blood cells
   C. is a basic part of blood
   D. is circulated through the body

22. When storing medical supplies, it is important to remember that liquids should be labeled

   A. only if the liquids are poisonous and there is the slightest chance that they will not be recognized
   B. whenever there is the slightest chance that they will not be recognized
   C. at all times, and discarded if labels have become detached
   D. only in those cases where the liquids will be given to patients

23. When dusting metal countertops in the clinic, it is BEST to use a clean cloth which is

   A. medicated   B. wet   C. dry   D. damp

24. Of the following statements concerning a hypodermic syringe, the one that is MOST correct is that a plunger

    A. used for taking blood specimens can be used with any syringe barrel
    B. can be used for any syringe barrel as long as it goes in easily
    C. can be used only with the syringe barrel that was made for it
    D. must be used with the syringe barrel that was made for it only if it is to be used for injections

25. The one of the following which should NOT be done when using a thermometer is to

    A. shake down the thermometer to 95F before taking the patient's temperature
    B. ask the patient to keep his lips closed when taking the temperature orally
    C. wash the thermometer in hot soapy water after use
    D. keep the thermometer in a container of alcohol when not in use

26. The temperature of an adult when taken by rectum is usually _____ than if taken _____ under the armpit.

    A. *higher;* either by mouth or
    B. *higher;* by mouth and lower than if taken
    C. *lower;* either by mouth or
    D. *lower;* by mouth and higher if taken

27. Of the following tests, the one which is associated with tuberculosis is the _____ test.

    A. Schick   B. Mantoux   C. Dick   D. Kahn

28. A needle that has been used to draw blood should be rinsed immediately after use in

    A. a disinfectant solution   B. hot water
    C. cold water   D. hot, soapy water

29. Of the following, the statement that is MOST correct is that a hypodermic needle should be checked for burrs, hooks, and sharpness

    A. once a week
    B. before it is sterilized
    C. after it has been sterilized
    D. after it has been used three or four times

30. The MOST accurate of the following statements is that, when a syringe and needle are being sterilized by boiling, the

    A. plunger must be completely out of the barrel
    B. needle should be left attached to the barrel as when in use
    C. plunger may be completely inside the barrel
    D. needle should be boiled at least twice as long as the syringe

31. Of the following, the MOST important reason for washing an instrument in hot soapy water is to

    A. sterilize the instrument
    B. destroy germs by heat
    C. destroy germs by coagulation
    D. remove foreign matter and bacteria

32. Assume that a hypodermic needle which is to be used for injection is accidentally brushed at the tip by your hand. Of the following, the action which should be taken before this needle is used is that it be

    A. washed under the hot water tap
    B. wiped with a sterile piece of gauze
    C. washed in hot soapy water, then rinsed in sterile water
    D. boiled for ten minutes

33. The CORRECT way to sterilize a scalpel is to

    A. place it in a chemical germicide
    B. boil it for 10 minutes
    C. put it in the autoclave
    D. pass it through a bright flame

34. Assume that a tray of instruments has been accidentally left uncovered for five minutes after it had been sterilized.
    Of the following, the action you should take to ensure that the instruments are sterile for use is to

    A. dip them in boiling water
    B. boil them for 10 minutes
    C. replace the cover on the tray
    D. wipe each instrument with sterile gauze

35. An intramuscular injection is MOST likely to be used in the administration of

    A. smallpox vaccine
    B. streptomycin
    C. glucose
    D. blood

36. The one of the following which is NOT a normal element of blood is

    A. hemoglobin
    B. a leucocyte
    C. marrow
    D. a platelet

37. Of the following statements regarding the Salk vaccine, the MOST accurate one is that it

    A. immunizes children and adults against paralytic poliomyelitis
    B. is a test to determine the presence of poliomyelitis virus in the blood
    C. is a test to determine whether a child is immune to poliomyelitis
    D. is used in the treatment of patients suffering from paralytic poliomyelitis

38. The GREATEST success in the treatment of cancer has been in cancer of the

    A. blood   B. stomach   C. liver   D. skin

39. An autopsy is a(n)

    A. type of blood test
    B. examination of tissue removed from a living organism
    C. examination of a human body after death
    D. test to determine the acidity of body fluids

40. The word *vascular* is MOST closely associated with

   A. the circulatory system
   B. respiration
   C. digestion
   D. the nervous system

41. The word *diagnosis* means MOST NEARLY

   A. preparation of a diagram
   B. determination of an illness
   C. medical examination of a patient
   D. written prescription

42. A tendon connects

   A. bone to bone
   B. muscle to bone
   C. muscle to muscle
   D. muscle to ligament

43. Blood takes on oxygen as it passes through the

   A. liver   B. heart   C. spleen   D. lungs

44. The fatty substance in the blood which is deposited in the artery walls and which is believed to cause hardening of the arteries is called

   A. amino acid   B. phenol   C. cholesterol   D. pectin

45. The digestive canal includes the

   A. stomach, small intestine, large intestine, and rectum
   B. stomach, larynx, large intestine, and rectum
   C. trachea, small intestine, large intestine, and rectum
   D. stomach, small intestine, large intestine, and abdominal cavity

46. When giving artificial respiration, it should be kept in mind that air is drawn into the lungs by the

   A. expansion of the chest cavity
   B. contraction of the chest cavity
   C. expansion of the lungs
   D. contraction of the lungs

47. The formula for converting degrees Centigrade to degrees Fahrenheit is as follows:
   Fahrenheit = 9/5 of Centigrade + 32°, or
   (multiply the number of degrees Centigrade by 9, divide by 5 and add 32)

   If the Centigrade thermometer reads 25°, the temperature, in degrees Fahrenheit, is

   A. 13   B. 45   C. 53   D. 77

48. To make a certain preparation, you have been told to mix one ounce of Liquid A and 3 ounces of Liquid B.
    If you have used 18 ounces of Liquid B in preparing a larger amount, the number of ounces of Liquid A you should use is

    A. 6 B. 15 C. 21 D. 54

49. If one inch is equal to approximately 2.5 centimeters, the number of inches in fifteen centimeters is MOST NEARLY

    A. 1.6 B. 6 C. 12.5 D. 37.5

Questions 50-52.

DIRECTIONS: Questions 50 through 52 are to be answered on the basis of the following situation.

you have been asked to keep records of the time spent with each patient by the doctors in the clinic where you are assigned, lour notes show that Dr. Jones spent the following amount of time with each patient he examined on a certain day:

Patient A - 14 minutes; Patient B - 13 minutes;
Patient C - 34 minutes; Patient D - 48 minutes;
Patient E - 26 minutes; Patient F - 20 minutes;
Patient G - 25 minutes.

50. The average number of minutes spent by Dr. Jones with each patient is MOST NEARLY

    A. 20 B. 25 C. 30 D. 35

51. If Dr. Jones is to take care of the seven patients mentioned above at one session, the number of hours he will have to remain at the clinic is MOST NEARLY _____ hour(s).

    A. 1 B. 2 C. 3 D. 4

52. The one of the following groups of patients that required the LEAST time to be examined is Patients

    A. A, C, and E
    C. C, E, and G
    B. B, D, and F
    D. A, D, and G

Questions 53-60.

DIRECTIONS: Questions 53 through 60 are to be answered on the basis of the usual rules of filing. Column I lists the names of 8 clinic patients. Column II lists the headings of file drawers into which you are to place the records of these patients. In the space at the right, corresponding to the names in Column I, print the letter preceding the heading of the file drawer in which the record should be filed.

COLUMN I

53. Thomas Adams
54. Joseph Albert
55. Frank Anaster
56. Charles Abt
57. John Alfred
58. Louis Aron
59. Francis Amos
60. William Adler

COLUMN II

A. Aab-Abi
B. Abj-Ach
C. Aci-Aco
D. Acp-Ada
E. Adb-Afr
F. Afs-Ago
G. Agp-Ahz
H. Aia-Ako
I. Akp-Ald
J. Ale-Amo
K. Amp-Aor
L. Aos-Apr
M. Aps-Asi
N. Asj-Ati
O. Atj-Awz

53.____
54.____
55.____
56.____
57.____
58.____
59.____
60.____

KEY (CORRECT ANSWERS)

1.	C	16.	D	31.	D	46.	A
2.	D	17.	C	32.	D	47.	D
3.	B	18.	B	33.	A	48.	A
4.	A	19.	B	34.	B	49.	B
5.	B	20.	A	35.	B	50.	B
6.	C	21.	A	36.	C	51.	C
7.	C	22.	C	37.	A	52.	A
8.	D	23.	D	38.	D	53.	D
9.	D	24.	C	39.	C	54.	I
10.	A	25.	C	40.	A	55.	K
11.	B	26.	A	41.	B	56.	B
12.	B	27.	B	42.	B	57.	J
13.	C	28.	C	43.	D	58.	M
14.	D	29.	B	44.	C	59.	J
15.	A	30.	A	45.	A	60.	E

TEST 2

DIRECTIONS: Each question or incomplete statement is followed by several suggested answers or completions. Select the one that BEST answers the question or completes the statement. *PRINT THE LETTER OF THE CORRECT ANSWER IN THE SPACE AT THE RIGHT.*

Questions 1-6.

DIRECTIONS: In answering Questions 1 through 6, alphabetize the four names listed in each question; then print in the space at the right the four letters preceding the alphabetized names to show the CORRECT alphabetical arrangement of the four names.

1. A. Frank Adam B. Frank Aarons 1.____
   C. Frank Aaron D. Frank Adams

2. A. Richard Lavine B. Richard Levine 2.____
   C. Edward Lawrence D. Edward Loraine

3. A. G. Frank Adam B. Frank Adam 3.____
   C. Fanny Adam D. Franklin Adam

4. A. George Cohn B. Richard Cohen 4.____
   C. Thomas Cohane D. George Cohan

5. A. Paul Shultz B. Robert Schmid 5.____
   C. Joseph Schwartz D. Edward Schmidt

6. A. Peter Consilazio B. Frank Consolezio 6.____
   C. Robert Consalizio D. Ella Consolizio

Questions 7-13.

DIRECTIONS: For Questions 7 through 13, select the letter preceding the word which means MOST NEARLY the same as the word in capital letters.

7. LEGIBLE 7.____

   A. readable B. eligible C. learned D. lawful

8. OBSERVE 8.____

   A. assist B. watch C. correct D. oppose

9. HABITUAL 9.____

   A. punctual B. occasional
   C. usual D. actual

10. CHRONOLOGICAL 10.____

    A. successive B. earlier
    C. later D. studious

11. ARREST
    A. punish   B. run   C. threaten   D. stop

12. ABSTAIN
    A. refrain   B. indulge   C. discolor   D. spoil

13. TOXIC
    A. poisonous   B. decaying
    C. taxing   D. defective

14. TOLERATE
    A. fear   B. forgive   C. allow   D. despise

15. VENTILATE
    A. vacate   B. air   C. extricate   D. heat

16. SUPERIOR
    A. perfect   B. subordinate
    C. lower   D. higher

17. EXTREMITY
    A. extent   B. limb   C. illness   D. execution

18. DIVULGED
    A. unrefined   B. secreted
    C. revealed   D. divided

19. SIPHON
    A. drain   B. drink   C. compute   D. discard

20. EXPIRATION
    A. trip   B. demonstration
    C. examination   D. end

Questions 21-40.

DIRECTIONS: Column I lists 20 words, numbered 21 through 40, which are used in medical practice. Column II lists words or phrases which describe the words in Column I. In the space at the right, next to the number of each of the words in Column I, place the letter preceding the words or phrases in Column II which BEST describes the word in Column I.

COLUMN I

21. Anemia
22. Anesthetic
23. Arthritis
24. Aseptic
25. Astigmatism
26. Catheter
27. Cranium
28. Diathermy
29. Enema
30. Electrocardiograph
31. Forceps
32. Gynecology
33. Lesion
34. Lumbago
35. Microscope
36. Obstetrics
37. Ophthalmology
38. Postnatal
39. Rabies
40. Stethoscope

COLUMN II

A. A tube used to drain fluid from the bladder
B. The skull
C. Inflammation of a joint
D. A fluid injected into the rectum for the purpose of clearing out the bowels
E. A drug used in surgery which makes one insensible to pain
F. Rheumatic pain in the back
G. The branch of medicine concerned with diseases of the eye
H. Examination of the inner parts of the body by use of x-rays and a special screen
I. free from disease germs
J. Deficiency of blood
K. The branch of medicine concerned with diseases of women
L. A tumorous growth
M. A structural defect of the eye
N. An apparatus for sterilization under pressurized steam
O. The shoulder blade
P. A type of treatment which depends upon production of heat in the tissues by high frequency current
Q. An instrument for recording electric changes caused by contraction of the muscles of the heart
R. An instrument for magnifying minute organisms
S. The branch of medicine concerned with the care and delivery of pregnant women
T. A wound or injury
U. An acute infectious disease which is transmitted by the bite of dogs and other animals
V. A band of tissue which connects bones or holds organs in place
W. A medication used to calm nerves
X. An instrument used to listen to sounds in the heart
Y. A pair of tongs
Z. Occurring after birth

21. ____
22. ____
23. ____
24. ____
25. ____
26. ____
27. ____
28. ____
29. ____
30. ____
31. ____
32. ____
33. ____
34. ____
35. ____
36. ____
37. ____
38. ____
39. ____
40. ____

KEY (CORRECT ANSWERS)

1.	C,B,A,D	11.	D	21.	J	31.	Y
2.	A,C,B,D	12.	A	22.	E	32.	K
3.	C,B,D,A	13.	A	23.	C	33.	T
4.	D,C,B,A	14.	C	24.	I	34.	F
5.	B,D,C,A	15.	B	25.	M	35.	R
6.	C,A,B,D	16.	D	26.	A	36.	S
7.	A	17.	B	27.	B	37.	G
8.	B	18.	C	28.	P	38.	Z
9.	C	19.	A	29.	D	39.	U
10.	A	20.	D	30.	Q	40.	X

PREPARING WRITTEN MATERIAL

PARAGRAPH REARRANGEMENT
COMMENTARY

The sentences that follow are in scrambled order. You are to rearrange them in proper order and indicate the letter choice containing the correct answer at the space at the right.

Each group of sentences in this section is actually a paragraph presented in scrambled order. Each sentence in the group has a place in that paragraph; no sentence is to be left out. You are to read each group of sentences and decide upon the best order in which to put the sentences so as to form a well-organized paragraph.

The questions in this section measure the ability to solve a problem when all the facts relevant to its solution are not given.

More specifically, certain positions of responsibility and authority require the employee to discover connection between events sometimes, apparently, unrelated. In order to do this, the employee will find it necessary to correctly infer that unspecified events have probably occurred or are likely to occur. This ability becomes especially important when action must be taken on incomplete information.

Accordingly, these questions require competitors to choose among several suggested alternatives, each of which presents a different sequential arrangement of the events. Competitors must choose the MOST logical of the suggested sequences.

In order to do so, they may be required to draw on general knowledge to infer missing concepts or events that are essential to sequencing the given events. Competitors should be careful to infer only what is essential to the sequence. The plausibility of the wrong alternatives will always require the inclusion of unlikely events or of additional chains of events which are NOT essential to sequencing the given events.

It's very important to remember that you are looking for the best of the four possible choices, and that the best choice of all may not even be one of the answers you're given to choose from.

There is no one right way to solve these problems. Many people have found it helpful to first write out the order of the sentences, as they would have arranged them, on their scrap paper before looking at the possible answers. If their optimum answer is there, this can save them some time. If it isn't, this method can still give insight into solving the problem. Others find it most helpful to just go through each of the possible choices, contrasting each as they go along. You should use whatever method feels comfortable and works for you.

While most of these types of questions are not that difficult, we've added a higher percentage of the difficult type, just to give you more practice. Usually there are only one or two questions on this section that contain such subtle distinctions that you're unable to answer confidently. And you then may find yourself stuck deciding between two possible choices, neither of which you're sure about.

EXAMINATION SECTION
TEST 1

DIRECTIONS: Each group of sentences in this section is actually a paragraph presented in scrambled order. Each sentence in the group has a place in that paragraph; no sentence is to be left out. You are to read each group of sentences, so as to form a well-organized paragraph. Before trying to answer the questions which follow each group of sentences, jot down the correct order of the sentences. Then answer each of the questions by printing the letter of the correct answer in the space at the right. Remember that you will receive credit only for answers marked.

P. The infant only feels the positive stimulation of warmth and food and does not differentiate the warmth and food from their source, mother.
Q. The infant, at the moment of birth, would feel the fear of dying if gracious fate did not preserve it from any awareness of the anxiety involved in the separation from mother.
R. The infant's state, then, is what has been called narcissism.
S. Mother is warmth, mother is food, mother is the euphoric state of satisfaction and security.
T. Even after being born, the infant is not yet aware of itself, and of the world as being outside of itself.

1. Which sentence did you put before Sentence Q?　　　　　　　　　　　　　　　　1._____

    A. P
    B. R
    C. S
    D. T
    E. None of the above. Sentence Q is first.

2. Which sentence did you put after Sentence S?　　　　　　　　　　　　　　　　　2._____

    A. P
    B. Q
    C. R
    D. T
    E. None of the above. Sentence S is last.

3. Which sentence did you put before Sentence P?　　　　　　　　　　　　　　　　3._____

    A. Q
    B. R
    C. S
    D. T
    E. None of the above. Sentence P is first.

2 (#1)

4. Which sentence did you put after Sentence P?

    A. Q
    B. R
    C. S
    D. T
    E. None of the above. Sentence P is last.

5. Which sentence did you put after Sentence R?

    A. P
    B. Q
    C. S
    D. T
    E. None of the above. Sentence R is last.

KEY (CORRECT ANSWERS)

1. E
2. C
3. D
4. C
5. E

TEST 2

DIRECTIONS: Each group of sentences in this section is actually a paragraph presented in scrambled order. Each sentence in the group has a place in that paragraph; no sentence is to be left out. You are to read each group of sentences, so as to form a well-organized paragraph. Before trying to answer the questions which follow each group of sentences, jot down the correct order of the sentences. Then answer each of the questions by printing the letter of the correct answer in the space at the right. Remember that you will receive credit only for answers marked.

    P. Then it requires knowledge and effort.
    Q. The former is my view.
    R. Or is love a pleasant sensation, something one *falls into* if one is lucky?
    S. The majority of people today, however, believe in the latter.
    T. Is love an art?

1. Which sentence did you put second?

   A. P   B. Q   C. R   D. S   E. T

2. Which sentence did you put after Sentence S?

   A. P
   B. Q
   C. R
   D. T
   E. None of the above. Sentence S is last.

3. Which sentence did you put before Sentence Q?

   A. P
   B. R
   C. S
   D. T
   E. None of the above. Sentence Q is first.

4. Which sentence did you put before Sentence P?

   A. Q
   B. R
   C. S
   D. T
   E. None of the above. Sentence P is first.

5. Which sentence did you put after Sentence Q?

   A. P
   B. R
   C. S
   D. T
   E. None of the above. Sentence Q is last.

KEY (CORRECT ANSWERS)

1. A
2. E
3. B
4. D
5. C

TEST 3

DIRECTIONS: Each group of sentences in this section is actually a paragraph presented in scrambled order. Each sentence in the group has a place in that paragraph; no sentence is to be left out. You are to read each group of sentences, so as to form a well-organized paragraph. Before trying to answer the questions which follow each group of sentences, jot down the correct order of the sentences. Then answer each of the questions by printing the letter of the correct answer in the space at the right. Remember that you will receive credit only for answers marked.

P. Indeed, in his time, Freud's theories of sex had a challenging and revolutionary character.
Q. Sexual mores have changed so much that Freud's theories no longer are shocking to the middle classes.
R. Freud has been criticized for his overevaluation of sex.
S. But what was true sixty years ago is no longer true.
T. This criticism resulted from a wish to remove an element from Freud's system which might arouse criticism among conventionally-minded people.

1. Which sentence did you put last?   1.____
   A. P   B. Q   C. R   D. S   E. T

2. Which sentence did you put before Sentence Q?   2.____
   A. P
   B. R
   C. S
   D. T
   E. None of the above. Sentence Q is first.

3. Which sentence did you put after Sentence T?   3.____
   A. P
   B. Q
   C. R
   D. S
   E. None of the above. Sentence T is last.

4. Which sentence did you put before Sentence R?   4.____
   A. P
   B. Q
   C. S
   D. T
   E. None of the above. Sentence R is first.

5. Which sentence did you put after Sentence R?   5.____
   A. P
   B. Q
   C. S
   D. T
   E. None of the above. Sentence R is last.

KEY (CORRECT ANSWERS)

1. B
2. C
3. A
4. E
5. D

TEST 4

DIRECTIONS: Each group of sentences in this section is actually a paragraph presented in scrambled order. Each sentence in the group has a place in that paragraph; no sentence is to be left out. You are to read each group of sentences, so as to form a well-organized paragraph. Before trying to answer the questions which follow each group of sentences, jot down the correct order of the sentences. Then answer each of the questions by printing the letter of the correct answer in the space at the right. Remember that you will receive credit only for answers marked.

- P. Early Scandanavian accounts, as well, are too mythological and legendary to serve as history.
- Q. The first trustworthy written evidence of a kingdom of Denmark belongs to the beginning of the Viking period.
- R. Ancient Roman knowledge of this remote country was fragmentary and unreliable.
- S. Archaeology and the study of place names, however, provide a certain amount of information about the earliest settlements.
- T. Everything before that is prehistory.

1. Which sentence did you put fourth?
   - A. P
   - B. B. Q
   - C. C. R
   - D. D. S
   - E. E. T

2. Which sentence did you put after Sentence T?
   - A. Q
   - B. R
   - C. S
   - D. None of the above. Sentence T is last.

3. Which sentence did you put after Sentence Q?
   - A. P
   - B. R
   - C. S
   - D. T
   - E. None of the above. Sentence Q is last.

4. Which sentence did you put before Sentence Q?
   - A. P
   - B. R
   - C. S
   - D. T
   - E. None of the above. Sentence Q is first.

5. Which sentence did you put after Sentence P?
   - A. Q
   - B. R
   - C. S
   - D. T
   - E. None of the above. Sentence P is last.

KEY (CORRECT ANSWERS)

1. A
2. C
3. D
4. E
5. C

TEST 5

DIRECTIONS: Each group of sentences in this section is actually a paragraph presented in scrambled order. Each sentence in the group has a place in that paragraph; no sentence is to be left out. You are to read each group of sentences, so as to form a well-organized paragraph. Before trying to answer the questions which follow each group of sentences, jot down the correct order of the sentences. Then answer each of the questions by printing the letter of the correct answer in the space at the right. Remember that you will receive credit only for answers marked.

P. In 1268, ambassadors were required to surrender all gifts they had received on their missions.
Q. In the 13th century, the Venetian republic began to lay down rules of conduct for its ambassadors.
R. In 1288, it was decreed that ambassadors were to report in writing on the results of their missions.
S. Such reports are a mine of historical material.
T. It is in Venice that the origins of modern diplomacy are to be sought.

1. Which sentence did you put second?
   A. P   B. Q   C. R   D. S   E. T

2. Which sentence did you put after Sentence R?
   A. P
   B. Q
   C. S
   D. T
   E. None of the above. Sentence R is last.

3. Which sentence did you put before Sentence P?
   A. Q
   B. R
   C. S
   D. T
   E. None of the above. Sentence P is first.

4. Which sentence did you put before Sentence T?
   A. P
   B. Q
   C. R
   D. S
   E. None of the above. Sentence T is first.

5. Which sentence did you put last?
   A. P   B. B. Q   C. C. R   D. D. S   E. E. T

95

KEY (CORRECT ANSWERS)

1. B
2. C
3. A
4. E
5. D

PREPARING WRITTEN MATERIAL
EXAMINATION SECTION
TEST 1

DIRECTIONS: Each question consists of a sentence which may or may not be an example of good English usage. Examine each sentence, considering grammar, punctuation, spelling, capitalization, and awkwardness. Then choose the correct statement about it from the four choices below it. If the English usage in the sentence given is better than any of the changes suggested in choices B, C, or D, pick choice A. (Do not pick a choice that will change the meaning of the sentence.) *PRINT THE LETTER OF THE CORRECT ANSWER IN THE SPACE AT THE RIGHT.*

1. We attended a staff conference on Wednesday the new safety and fire rules were discussed.   1.____
   A. This is an example of acceptable writing.
   B. The words "safety," "fire," and "rules" should begin with capital letters.
   C. There should be a comma after the word "Wednesday."
   D. There should be a period after the word "Wednesday" and the word "the" should begin with a capital letter.

2. Neither the dictionary or the telephone directory could be found in the office library.   2.____
   A. This is an example of acceptable writing.
   B. The word "or" should be changed to "nor."
   C. The word "library" should be spelled "libery."
   D. The word "neither" should be changed to "either."

3. The report would have been typed correctly if the typist could read the draft.   3.____
   A. This is an example of acceptable writing.
   B. The word "would" should be removed.
   C. The word "have" should be inserted after the word "could."
   D. The word "correctly" should be changed to "correct."

4. The supervisor brought the reports and forms to an employees desk.   4.____
   A. This is an example of acceptable writing.
   B. The word "brought" should be changed to "took."
   C. There should be a comma after the word "reports" and a comma after the word "forms."
   D. The word "employees" should be spelled "employee's."

5. It's important for all the office personnel to submit their vacation schedules on time.   5.____
   A. This is an example of acceptable writing.
   B. The word "It's" should be spelled "Its."
   C. The word "their" should be spelled "they're."
   D. The word "personnel" should be spelled "personal."

6. The report, along with the accompanying documents, were submitted for review.
   A. This is an example of acceptable writing.
   B. The words "were submitted" should be changed to "was submitted."
   C. The word "accompanying" should be spelled "accompaning."
   D. The comma after the word "report" should be taken out.

7. If others must use your files, be certain that they understand how the system works, but insist that you do all the filing and refiling.
   A. This is an example of acceptable writing.
   B. There should be a period after the word "works," and the word "but" should start a new sentence.
   C. The words "filing" and "refiling" should be spelled "fileing" and "refileing."
   D. There should be a comma after the word "but."

8. The appeal was not considered because of its late arrival.
   A. This is an example of acceptable writing.
   B. The word "its" should be changed to "it's."
   C. The word "its" should be changed to "the."
   D. The words "late arrival" should be changed to "arrival late."

9. The letter must be read carefuly to determine under which subject it should be filed.
   A. This is an example of acceptable writing.
   B. The word "under" should be changed to "at."
   C. The word "determine" should be spelled "determin."
   D. The word "carefuly" should be spelled "carefully."

10. He showed potential as an office manager, but he lacked skill in delegating work.
    A. This is an example of acceptable writing.
    B. The word "delegating" should be spelled "delagating."
    C. The word "potential" should be spelled "potencial."
    D. The words "he lacked" should be changed to "was lacking."

KEY (CORRECT ANSWERS)

1.	D	6.	B
2.	B	7.	A
3.	C	8.	A
4.	D	9.	D
5.	A	10.	A

TEST 2

DIRECTIONS: Each question consists of a sentence which may or may not be an example of good English usage. Examine each sentence, considering grammar, punctuation, spelling, capitalization, and awkwardness. Then choose the correct statement about it from the four choices below it. If the English usage in the sentence given is better than any of the changes suggested in choices B, C, or D, pick choice A. (Do not pick a choice that will change the meaning of the sentence.) *PRINT THE LETTER OF THE CORRECT ANSWER IN THE SPACE AT THE RIGHT.*

1. The supervisor wants that all staff members report to the office at 9:00 A.M.   1.____
    A. This is an example of acceptable writing.
    B. The word "that" should be removed and the word "to" should be inserted after the word "members."
    C. There should be a comma after the word "wants" and a comma after the word "office."
    D. The word "wants" should be changed to "want" and the word "shall" should be inserted after the word "members."

2. Every morning the clerk opens the office mail and distributes it.   2.____
    A. This is an example of acceptable writing.
    B. The word "opens" should be changed to "open."
    C. The word "mail" should be changed to "letters."
    D. The word "it" should be changed to "them."

3. The secretary typed more fast on a desktop computer than on a laptop computer.   3.____
    A. This is an example of acceptable writing.
    B. The words "more fast" should be changed to "faster."
    C. There should be a comma after the words "desktop computer."
    D. The word "than" should be changed to "then."

4. The new stenographer needed a desk a computer, a chair and a blotter.   4.____
    A. This is an example of acceptable writing.
    B. The word "blotter" should be spelled "blodder."
    C. The word "stenographer" should begin with a capital letter.
    D. There should be a comma after the word "desk."

5. The recruiting officer said, "There are many different goverment jobs available."   5.____
    A. This is an example of acceptable writing.
    B. The word "There" should not be capitalized.
    C. The word "government" should be spelled "government."
    D. The comma after the word "said" should be removed.

6. He can recommend a mechanic whose work is reliable.   6.____
    A. This is an example of acceptable writing.
    B. The word "reliable" should be spelled "relyable."
    C. The word "whose" should be spelled "who's."
    D. The word "mechanic should be spelled "mecanic."

7. She typed quickly; like someone who had not a moment to lose.
   A. This is an example of acceptable writing.
   B. The word "not" should be removed.
   C. The semicolon should be changed to a comma.
   D. The word "quickly" should be placed before instead of after the word "typed."

8. She insisted that she had to much work to do.
   A. This is an example of acceptable writing.
   B. The word "insisted" should be spelled "incisted."
   C. The word "to" used in front of "much" should be spelled "too."
   D. The word "do" should be changed to "be done."

9. He excepted praise from his supervisor for a job well done.
   A. This is an example of acceptable writing.
   B. The word "excepted" should be spelled "accepted."
   C. The order of the words "well done" should be changed to "done well."
   D. There should be a comma after the word "supervisor."

10. What appears to be intentional errors in grammar occur several times in the passage.
    A. This is an example of acceptable writing.
    B. The word "occur" should be spelled "occurr."
    C. The word "appears" should be changed to "appear."
    D. The phrase "several times" should be changed to "from time to time."

KEY (CORRECT ANSWERS)

1. B   6. A
2. A   7. C
3. B   8. C
4. D   9. B
5. C   10. C

TEST 3

DIRECTIONS: Each question consists of a sentence which may or may not be an example of good English usage. Examine each sentence, considering grammar, punctuation, spelling, capitalization, and awkwardness. Then choose the correct statement about it from the four choices below it. If the English usage in the sentence given is better than any of the changes suggested in choices B, C, or D, pick choice A. (Do not pick a choice that will change the meaning of the sentence.) *PRINT THE LETTER OF THE CORRECT ANSWER IN THE SPACE AT THE RIGHT.*

1. The clerk could have completed the assignment on time if he knows where these materials were located.
   A. This is an example of acceptable writing.
   B. The word "knows" should be replaced by "had known."
   C. The word "were" should be replaced by "had been."
   D. The words "where these materials were located" should be replaced by "the location of these materials."

   1._____

2. All employees should be given safety training. Not just those who accidents.
   A. This is an example of acceptable writing.
   B. The period after the word "training" should be changed to a colon.
   C. The period after the word "training" should be changed to a semicolon, and the first letter of the word "Not" should be changed to a small "n."
   D. The period after the word "training" should be changed to a comma, and the first letter of the word "Not" should be changed to a small "n."

   2._____

3. This proposal is designed to promote employee awareness of the suggestion program, to encourage employee participation in the program, and to increase the number of suggestions submitted.
   A. This is an example of acceptable writing.
   B. The word "proposal" should be spelled "proposal."
   C. The words "to increase the number of suggestions submitted" should be changed to "an increase in the number of suggestions is expected."
   D. The word "promote" should be changed to "enhance" and the word "increase" should be changed to "add to."

   3._____

4. The introduction of inovative managerial techniques should be preceded by careful analysis of the specific circumstances and conditions in each department.
   A. This is an example of acceptable writing.
   B. The word "technique" should be spelled "techneques."
   C. The word "inovative" should be spelled "innovative."
   D. A comma should be placed after the word "circumstances" and after the word "conditions."

   4._____

101

5. This occurrence indicates that such criticism embarrasses him.
   A. This is an example of acceptable writing.
   B. The word "occurrence" should be spelled "occurence."
   C. The word "criticism" should be spelled "critisism.
   D. The word "embarrasses" should be spelled "embarasses.

KEY (CORRECT ANSWERS)

1. B
2. D
3. A
4. C
5. A

GLOSSARY OF LEGAL, MEDICAL, SOCIAL WORK TERMS

TABLE OF CONTENTS

	Page
Abandonment ... Advocacy	1
Affidavit ... Annual Review of Dependency Cases	2
Anomie ... Battery	3
Best Interests of the Child ... Caretaker	4
Cartilage ... Child Abuse	5
Child Abuse and Neglect	6
Child Abuse Prevention and Treatment Act ... Child Health Visitor	7
Child in Need of Supervision ... Child Welfare League of America	8
Child Welfare Resource Information Exchange ... Circumstantial Evidence	9
Civil Proceeding ... Community Organization	10
Community Support Systems	11
Compliance ... Corporal Punishment	12
Cortex ... Custody	13
Custody Hearing ... Denver Model	14
Dependency ... Discipline	15
Dislocation ... Due Process	16
Duodenum ... Evidence	17
Exhibit ... Expungement	18
Extravasated Blood ... Family Dynamics	19
Family Dysfunction ... Family Violence	20
Federal Regulations ... Fracture	21
Frontal ... Helpline	22
Hematemesis ... Hypovitaminosis	23
Identification of Child Abuse and Neglect ... Incest	24
Incidence ... Infanticide	25
Institutional Child Abuse and Neglect ... Juvenile Judge	27
Labeling ... Legal Rights of Persons Identified in Reports	28
Lesion ... Local Authority	29
Long Bone ... Maternal Characteristics Scale	30
Maternal-Infant Bonding ... Model Child Protection Act	31
Mondale Act ... National Center for the Prevention and Treatment of Child Abuse and Neglect	32
National Center on Child Abuse and Neglect ... National Committee for the Prevention of Child Abuse	33
National Register ... Nurturance	34
Occipital ... Parent Effectiveness Training	35
Parental Stress Services ... Pathognomonic	36
Perinatal ... Pre-trial Diversion	37

TABLE OF CONTENTS
(Continued)

Prevention of Child Abuse and Neglect ... Probation	38
Program Coordination ... Public Defender	39
Public Law 93-247 ... Regional Resource Center	40
Registry ... Res Ipsa Loquitor	41
Retina ... Self-Incrimination	42
Sentencing ... Social Assessment	43
Social History ... Societal Child Abuse and Neglect	44
Special Child ... State Authority	45
Status Offense ... Subdural Hematoma	46
Subpoena ... Surrogate Parent	47
Suspected Child Abuse and Neglect ... Trauma	48
Trauma X ... Vascular	49
Venereal Disease ... Willful	50
Witness ... X-Rays	51
ACRONYMS	52

GLOSSARY OF
Legal, Medical, Social Work Terms

ABANDONMENT
Act of a parent or caretaker leaving a child without adequate supervision or provision for his/her needs for an excessive period of time. State laws vary in defining adequacy of supervision and the length of time a child may be left alone or in the care of another before abandonment is determined. The age of the child also is an important factor. In legal terminology, "abandonment cases" are suits calling for the termination of parental rights.

ABDOMINAL DISTENTION
Swelling of the stomach area. The distention may be caused by internal injury or obstruction or by malnutrition.

ABRASION
Wound in which an area of the body surface is scraped of skin or mucous membrane.

ABUSE (See CHILD ABUSE AND NEGLECT)

ABUSED CHILD (See INDICATORS OF CHILD ABUSE AND NEGLECT)

ABUSED PARENT
Parent who has been abused as a child and who therefore may be more likely to abuse his/her own child.

ABUSER, PASSIVE (See PASSIVE ABUSER)

ACADEMY OF CERTIFIED SOCIAL WORKERS (ACSW)
Professional category identifying experienced social workers. Eligibility is determined by written examination following two years' full-time or 3,000 hours part-time paid post-Master's degree experience and continuous National Association of Social Workers (NASW) membership.

ACTING OUT
1) Behavior of an abusive parent who may be unconsciously and indirectly expressing anger toward his/her own parents or other significant person.
2) Aggressive or sexual behavior explained by some psychoanalytic theorists as carrying out fantasies or expressing unconscious feelings and conflicts.
3) Children's play or play therapy activities used as a means of expressing hitherto repressed feelings.

ACUTE CARE CAPACITY
Capacity of a community to respond quickly and responsibly to a report of a child abuse or neglect. It involves receiving the report and providing a diagnostic assessment including both a medical assessment and an evaluation of family dynamics. It also involves rapid intervention, including immediate protection of the child when needed and referral for long term care or service to the child and his/her family.

ADJUDICATION HEARING
Court hearing in which it is decided whether or not charges against a parent or caretaker are substantiated by admissible evidence. Also known as jurisdictional or evidentiary hearing.

ADMISSIBLE EVIDENCE
Evidence which may be legally and properly used in court. (See also EVIDENCE, EVIDENTIARY STANDARDS, EXPERT TESTIMONY)

ADVOCACY
Interventive strategy in which a helping person assumes an active role in assisting or supporting a specific child and/or family or a cause on behalf of children and/or families. This could involve finding and facilitating services for specific cases or developing new

services or promoting program coordination. The advocate uses his/her power to meet client needs or to promote causes.

AFFIDAVIT
Written statement signed in the presence of a Notary Public who "swears in" the signer. The contents of the affidavit are stated under penalty of perjury. Affidavits are frequently used in the initiation of juvenile court cases and are, at times, presented to the court as evidence.

AGAINST MEDICAL ADVICE (AMA)
Going against the orders of a physician. In cases of child abuse or neglect, this usually means the removal of a child from a hospital without the physician's consent.

AID TO FAMILIES WITH DEPENDENT CHILDREN (AFDC) (See SOCIAL SECURITY ACT)

ALLEGATION
An assertion, declaration, or statement of a party to a legal action, which sets out what he or she expects to prove. In a child abuse or neglect case, the allegation forms the basis of the petition or accusation containing charges of specific acts of maltreatment which the petitioner hopes to prove at the trial.

ALOPECIA
Absence of hair from skin areas where it normally appears; baldness.

AMERICAN ACADEMY OF PEDIATRICS (AAP)
P.O. Box 1034
Evanston, Illinois 60204
AAP is the pan-American association of physicians certified in the care of infants, children, and adolescents. It was founded in 1930 for the primary purpose of ensuring "the attainment of all children of the Americas of their full potential for physical, emotional, and social health." Services and activities of AAP include standards-setting for pediatric residencies, scholarships, continuing education, standards-setting for child health care, community health services, consultation, publications, and research.

AMERICAN HUMANE ASSOCIATION, CHILDREN'S DIVISION (AHA)
5351 S. Roslyn St.
Englewood, Colorado 80110
National association of individuals and agencies working to prevent neglect, abuse, and exploitation of children. Its objectives are to inform the public of the problem, to promote understanding of its causes, to advise on the identification and protection of abused and neglected children, and to assist in organizing new and improving existing child protection programs and services. Some of the programs and services of CDAHA include research, consultation and surveys, legislative guidance, staff development training and workshops, and publications. AHA includes an Animal Division in addition to the Children's Division.

AMERICAN PUBLIC WELFARE ASSOCIATION (APWA)
1125 Fifteenth St. N.W. Suite 300
Washington, D.C. 20005
APWA was founded in 1930 and has, from its inception, been a voluntary membership organization composed of individuals and agencies interested in issues of public welfare. National in scope, its dual purpose is to: 1) exert a positive influence on the shaping of national social policy, and 2) promote professional development of persons working in the area of public welfare. APWA sponsors an extensive program of policy analysis and research, testimony and consultation, publications, conferences, and workshops. It works for policies which are more equitable, less complex, and easier to administer in order that public welfare personnel can respond efficiently and effectively to the needs of persons they serve.

ANNUAL REVIEW OF DEPENDENCY CASES
Annual or other periodic reviews of dependency cases to determine whether continued

child placement or court supervision of a child is necessary. Increasingly required by state law, such reviews by the court also provide some judicial supervision of probation or casework services.

ANOMIE
A state of anomie is characterized by attitudes of aimlessness, futility, and lack of motivation and results from the breakdown or failure of standards, rules, norms, and values that ordinarily bind people together in some socially organized way.

ANOREXIA
Lack or loss of appetite for food.

APATHY-FUTILITY SYNDROME
Immature personality type often associated with child neglect and characterized by an inability to feel and to find any significant meaning in life. This syndrome, often arising from early deprivations in childhood, is frequently perpetuated from generation to generation within a family system. (Polansky)

APPEAL
Resort to a higher court in an attempt to have a decision or ruling of the lower court corrected or reversed because of some claimed error or injustice. Appeals follow several different formats. Occasionally, appeals will result in a rehearing of the entire case. Usually, however, appeals are limited to consideration of questions of whether the lower court judge correctly applied the law to the facts of the case.

ASSESSMENT
1) Determination of the validity of a reported case of suspected child abuse or neglect through investigatory interviews with persons involved. This could include interviews with the family, the child, school, and neighbors, as well as with other professionals and paraprofessionals having direct contact with the child or family.
2) Determination of the treatment potential and treatment plan for confirmed cases.

ASSAULT
Intentional or reckless threat of physical injury to a person. Aggravated assault is committed with the intention of carrying out the threat or other crimes. Simple assault is committed without the intention of carrying out the threat or if the attempt at injury is not completed. (See also BATTERY, SEXUAL ASSAULT)

ATROPHY
Wasting away of flesh, tissue, cell, or organ.

AVITAMINOSIS
Condition due to complete lack of one or more essential vitamins. (See also HYPOVITAMINOSIS)

BATTERED CHILD SYNDROME
Term introduced in 1962 by C. Henry Kempe, M.D., in the *Journal of the American Medical Association* in an article describing a combination of physical and other signs indicating that a child's internal and/or external injuries result from acts committed by a parent or caretaker. In some states, the battered child syndrome has been judicially recognized as an accepted medical diagnosis. Frequently this term is misused or misunderstood as the only type of child abuse and neglect. (See also CHILD ABUSE AND NEGLECT)

BATTERED WOMEN
Women who are victims of non-accidental physical and/or psychological injury inflected by a spouse or mate. There seems to be a relationship between child abuse and battered women, with both often occurring in the same family. (See also SPOUSE ABUSE)

BATTERY
Offensive contact or physical violence with a person without his/her consent, and which may or may not be preceded by a threat of assault. Because a minor cannot legally give consent, any such contact or violence against a child is considered battery. The action may be aggravated, meaning intentional, or it may be simple, meaning that the action was not intentional or did not cause

severe harm. Assault is occasionally used to mean attempted battery. (See also ASSAULT)

BEST INTERESTS OF THE CHILD
Standard for deciding among alternative plans for abused or neglected children. This is also known as the least detrimental alternative principle. Usually it is assumed that it is in the child's best interest and least detrimental if the child remains in the home, provided that the parents can respond to treatment. However, the parents' potential for treatment may be difficult to assess and it may not be known whether the necessary resources are available. A few authorities believe that except where the child's life is in danger, it is always in the child's best interest to remain in the home. This view reflects the position that in evaluating the least detrimental alternative and the child's best interest, the child's psychological as well as physical well-being must be considered. In developing a plan, the best interest of the child may not be served because of parents' legal rights or because agency policy and practice focuses on foster care. The best interest of the child and least detrimental alternative principles were articulated as a reaction to the overuse of child placement in cases of abuse and neglect. Whereas "best interest of the child" suggests that some placement may be justified, "least detrimental alternative" is stronger in suggesting that any placement or alternative can have some negative consequences and should be monitored.

BEYOND A REASONABLE DOUBT (See EVIDENTIARY STANDARDS)

BONDING
The psychological attachment of mother to child which develops during and immediately following childbirth. Bonding, which appears to be crucial to the development of a health parent/child relationship, may be studied during and immediately following delivery to help identify potential families-at-risk. Bonding is normally a natural occurrence but it may be disrupted by separation of mother and baby or by situational or psychological factors causing the mother to reject the baby at birth.

BRUISE (See INTRADERMAL HEMORRHAGE)

BURDEN OF PROOF
The duty, usually falling on the state as petitioner in a child maltreatment case, of producing evidence at a trial so as to establish the truth of the allegations against the parent. At the commencement of a trial, it is always up to the petitioner to first present evidence which proves their case. (See also EVIDENCE, EVIDENTIARY STANDARDS)

BURN
Wound resulting from the application of too much heat. Burns are classified by the degree of damage caused.
    1st degree: Scorching or painful redness of the skin.
    2nd degree: Formation of blisters.
    3rd degree: Destruction of outer layers of the skin.

BURN OUT (See staff burn out.)

CALCIFICATION
Formation of bone. The amount of calcium deposited can indicate via X-ray the degree of healing of a broken bone or the location of previous fractures which have healed prior to the X-ray.

CALLUS
New bone formed during the healing process of a fracture.

CALVARIUM
Dome-like portion of the skull.

CARETAKER
A person responsible for a child's health or welfare, including the child's parent, guardian, or other person within the child's own home; or a person responsible for a child's health or welfare in a relative's home, foster care home, or residential institution. A caretaker is responsible for meeting a child's

basic physical and psychological needs and for providing protection and supervision.

CARTILAGE
The hard connective tissue that is not bone but, in the unborn and growing child, may be the forerunner of bone before calcium is deposited in it.

CASE MANAGEMENT
Coordination of the multiplicity of services required by a child abuse and neglect client. Some of these services may be purchased from an agency other than the mandated agency. In general, the role of the case manager is not the provision of direct services but the monitoring of those services to assure that they are relevant to the client, delivered in a useful way, and appropriately used by the client. To do this, a case manager assumes the following responsibilities.
1) Ascertains that all mandated reports have been properly filed.
2) Informs all professionals involved with the family that reports of suspected child abuse or neglect have been made.
3) Keeps all involved workers apprised of new information.
4) Calls and chairs the intial case conference for assessment, disposition, and treatment plans; conference may include parents, physician, probation worker, police, public health nurse, private therapist, parent aide, protective service and welfare workers, or others.
5) Coordinates interagency follow-up.
6) Calls further case conferences as needed. (See also PURCHASE OF SERVICE)

CASEWORK
A method of social work intervention which helps an individual or family improve their functioning in society by changing both internal attitudes and feelings and external circumstances directly affecting the individual or family. This contrasts with community organization and other methods of social work intervention which focuses on changing institutions or society. Social casework relies on a relationship between the worker and client as the primary tool for effecting change.

CATEGORICAL AID
Government financial assistance given to individuals who are aged or disabled or to families with dependent children. The eligibility requirements and financial assistance vary for different categories of persons, according to the guidelines of the Social Security Act. (See also SOCIAL SECURITY ACT)

CENTRAL REGISTER
Records of child abuse reports collected centrally from various agencies under state law or voluntary agreement. Agencies receiving reports of suspected abuse check with the central register to determine whether prior reports have been received by other agencies concerning the same child or parents. The purposes of central registers may be to alert authorities to families with a prior history of abuse, to assist agencies in planning for abusive families, and to provide data for statistical analysis of child abuse. Due to variance in state laws for reporting child abuse and neglect, there are diverse methods of compiling these records and of access to them. Although access to register records is usually restricted, critics warn of confidentiality problems and the importance of expunging unverified reports. (See also EXPUNGEMENT)

CHILD
A person, also known as minor, from birth to legal age of maturity for whom a parent and/or caretaker, foster parent, public or private home, institution, or agency is legally responsible. The 1974 Child Abuse Prevention and Treatment Act defines a child as a person under 18. In some states, a person of any age with a developmental disability is defined as a child.

CHILD ABUSE (See CHILD ABUSE AND NEGLECT)

CHILD ABUSE AND NEGLECT (CAN)
All-inclusive term, as defined in the Child Abuse Prevention and Treatment Act, for "the physical or mental injury, sexual abuse, negligent treatment or maltreatment of a child under the age of eighteen by a person who is responsible for the child's welfare. There is agreement that some parental care and supervision is essential, there is disagreement as to how much is necessary for a minimally acceptable environment.

Child Abuse refers specifically to an act of commission by a parent or caretaker which is not accidental and harms or threatens to harm a child's physical or mental health or welfare. All 50 States have a child abuse reporting law with varying definitions of child abuse and varying provisions as to who must and may report, penalties for not reporting, and required agency action following the report. Factors such as the age of the child and the severity of injury are important in determining abuse.

Physical Abuse
Child abuse which results in physical injury, including fractures, burns, bruises, welts, cuts, and/or internal injuries. Physical abuse often occurs in the name of discipline or punishment, and ranges from a slap of the hand to use of objects such as straps, belts, kitchen utensils, pipes, etc. (See also BATTERED CHILD SYNDROME)

Psychological/Emotional Abuse
Child abuse which results in impaired psychological growth and development. Frequently occurs as verbal abuse or excessive demands on a child's performance and results in a negative self-image on the part of the child and disturbed child behavior. May occur with or without physical abuse.

Sexual Abuse
Child abuse which results in any act of a sexual nature upon or with a child. Most states define any sexual involvement of a parent or caretaker with a child as a sexual act and therefore abuse. The most common form is incest between fathers and daughters.

Verbal Abuse
A particular form of psychological/emotional abuse characterized by constant verbal harassment and denigration of a child. Many persons abused as children report feeling more permanently damaged by verbal abuse than by isolated or repeated experiences of physical abuse.

Child Neglect refers to an act of omission, specifically the failure of a parent or other person legally responsible for a child's welfare to provide for the child's basic needs and proper level of care with respect to food, clothing, shelter, hygiene, medical attention, or supervision. Most states have neglect and/or dependency statutes; however, not all states require the reporting of neglect. While there is agreement that some parental care and supervision is essential, there is disagreement as to how much is necessary for a minimally acceptable environment. Severe neglect sometimes occurs because a parent is apathetic, impulse-ridden, mentally retarded, depressed, or psychotic.

Educational Neglect
Failure to provide for a child's cognitive development. This may include failure to conform to state legal requirements regarding school attendance.

Medical Neglect
Failure to seek medical or dental treatment for a health problem or condition which, if untreated, could become severe enough to represent a danger to the child. Except among religious sects prohibiting medical treatment, medical neglect is usually only one part of a larger family problem.

Moral Neglect
Failure to give a child adequate guidance in developing positive social values, such as parents who allow or teach their children to steal.

Physical Neglect
Failure to provide for a child's basic survival needs, such as food, clothing, shelter, and supervision, to the extent that the failure represents a hazard to the child's health or safety. Determining neglect for lack of supervision depends upon the child's age and competence, the amount of unsupervised time, the time of day when the child is unsupervised, and the degree of parental planning for the unsupervised period. For a particular kind of physical neglect involving failure to feed a baby or small child sufficiently, see FAILURE TO THRIVE SYNDROME.

Psychological /Emotional Neglect
Failure to provide the psychological nurturance necessary for a child's psychological growth and development. It is usually very difficult to prove the cause and effect relationship between the parent's unresponsiveness and lack of nurturance and the child's symptoms, and many states do not include psychological or emotional neglect in their reporting laws.

CHILD ABUSE PREVENTION AND TREATMENT ACT (PUBLIC LAW 93-247)
Act introduced and promoted in Congress by then U.S. Senator Walter Mondale and signed into law on January 31, 1974. The act established the National Center on Child Abuse and Neglect in the HEW Children's Bureau and authorized annual appropriations of between $15 million and $25 million through Fiscal Year 1977, but it is anticipated that Congress will extend the act for several years. Actual appropriations have been less than authorized. The purpose of the National Center is to conduct and compile research, provide an information clearinghouse, compile and publish training materials, provide technical assistance, investigate national incidence, and fund demonstration projects related to prevention, identification, and treatment of child abuse and neglect. In the 1974 act, not more than 20% of the appropriated funds may be used for direct assistance to states, which must be in compliance with specific legislative requirements including, among others, reporting and investigation of suspected neglect as well as abuse, provision of multidisciplinary programs, and appointment of a *guardian ad litem* to represent the child in all judicial proceedings. The act emphasizes multidisciplinary approaches. It also provides for funding for parent self-help projects.

Many persons do not understand that this act is primarily to support research and demonstration projects. Much larger amounts of funding for the ongoing provisions of child abuse and neglect services are provided to states through Title IV-B and Title XX of the Social Security Act.

CHILD DEVELOPMENT
Pattern of sequential stages of interrelated physical, psychological, and social development in the process of maturation from infancy and total dependence to adulthood and relative independence. Parents need to understand the level of maturity consistent with each stage of development and should not expect a child to display a level of maturity of which the child is incapable at a particular stage. Abusive or neglectful parents frequently impair a child's healthy growth and development because they do not understand child development or are otherwise unable to meet the child's physical, social, and psychological needs at a given stage or stages of development.

CHILD HEALTH VISITOR
Professional or paraprofessional who visits a home shortly after the birth of a baby and periodically thereafter to identify current and potential child health and development and family stress problems and to facilitate use of needed community services. While currently operating in many European countries, child health visitor programs are rare in the U.S. because they are perceived as contrary to the right to privacy and parental rights. A universal mandatory child health visitor program has, however, been recommended by several

authorities as the most effective way to assure children's rights and prevent child abuse and neglect. Also known as Home Health Visitor.

CHILD IN NEED OF SUPERVISION
Juvenile who has committed a delinquent act and has been found by a children's court judge to require further court supervision, such as 1) probation, or 2) the transfer of custody of the child to a relative or public or private welfare agency for a period of time, usually not to exceed one year. Also known as Person in Need of Supervision (PINS) or Minor in Need of Supervision (MINS).

CHILD NEGLECT (See CHILD ABUSE AND NEGLECT)

CHILD PORNOGRAPHY
The obscene or pornographic photography, filming, or depiction of children for commercial purposes. Recent campaigns have begun to increase public awareness of this problem. Also as a result of public pressure against these materials, the federal government and some states are currently implementing special legislation to outlaw the sale and interstate transportation of pornographic materials that portray children engaged in explicit sexual acts.

CHILD PROSTITUTION
Legislation prohibiting the use of children as prostitutes is currently being implemented by the federal government and many states. The use of or participation by children in sexual acts with adults for reward or financial gain when no force is present.

CHILD PROTECTIVE SERVICES or CHILD PROTECTION SERVICES (CPS)
A specialized child welfare service, usually part of a county department of public welfare, legally responsible in most states for investigating suspected cases of child abuse and neglect and intervening in confirmed cases. Qualifications of CPS workers vary, with some counties employing CPS workers without prior human services training and others requiring at least a , Bachelor's degree in social work. With over 3,000 counties in the U.S., there are many kinds of CPS programs of varying quality. Common to most is the problem of insufficient staff overburdened with excessive caseloads. This plus the pressure of CPS work creates stress for many CPS staff. (See also STAFF BURNOUT, STAFF FLIGHT, and STAFF SATISFACTION)

CHILD WELFARE AGENCY
A public or voluntary agency providing service to children in their own homes and/or in day care, and which may be licensed to place children in foster homes, group homes, or institutions or into permanent adoptive homes. The number of children served annually by child welfare agencies in the U.S. is estimated to be over one million, the majority being served by public agencies. Payments for foster care represent well over half the total of child welfare agencies' expenditures.

Child welfare agencies which meet certain standards, including Standards for Protective Services, are accredited by the Child Welfare League of America. It is estimated that the majority of social workers employed by these accredited agencies hold a Master's degree. In public child welfare agencies, Master's degree social workers are a minority, with specific educational requirements varying from state to state. However, unlike many other fields of social work which share responsibility with other professions, child welfare is a domain for which social work has been accorded major responsibility. Believing that child protection is a public child welfare agency responsibility, few private agencies provide it.

CHILD WELFARE LEAGUE OF AMERICA (CWLA)
67 Irving Place
New York,
N.Y. 10003
Founded in 1920, the Child Welfare League of America is a privately supported, non-sectarian organization which is dedicated to the improvement of care and services for

deprived, neglected, and dependent children and their families. Its program is directed toward helping agencies and communities in the U.S. and Canada to provide essential social services to promote the well-being of children. CWLA is an advocate for children and families, a clearinghouse and forum for knowledge and experience of persons in the field, and a coordinating facility through which all concerned with child welfare can share their efforts. Programs of the League and its membership of over 300 affiliated public and private agencies include: accreditation of agencies, adoption services, conferences, consultation, training, library/information services, publications, personnel services, public affairs and legislative programs, standards development, and surveys.

CHILD WELFARE RESOURCE INFORMATION EXCHANGE
A project of the Children's Bureau of the Administration for Children, Youth and Families, HEW. It is a source for materials on exemplary programs, curricula, technologies, and methods which ahve brought more effective and efficient services to children. Its purpose is to improve the delivery of child welfare services by identifying successful programs, methods, research, and materials, and by assisting agencies in adapting them for their own use. The Exchange disseminates information it has gathered through abstracts, a bimonthly bulletin, regional workshops, and colloquia.

CHILDHOOD LEVEL OF LIVING SCALE (CLL)
Instrument used to measure the level of physical and emotional/cognitive care a child is receiving in his/her home. Rated are adequacy of food, clothing, furniture, etc., as well as evidence of affection, type of discipline, and cultural stimulation. The scale is designed to be used as a guide to assessing nurturance levels rather than as objective evidence of neglect.

CHILDREN-AT-RISK
May refer to the possibility that children in the custody of a state or county will get lost in a series of placements or for other reasons not be returned to their natural homes when these homes are no longer threatening to the children's welfare. May also refer to children in potentially abusive institutions, but usually refer to children in families-at-risk. (See also FAMILIES-AT-RISK)

CHILDREN'S DEFENSE FUND (CDF) 1520 New Hampshire Ave., N.W. Washington, D.C. 20036
A non-profit organization founded in 1973. Staff includes researchers, lawyers, and others dedicated to long-range and systematic advocacy on behalf of children. CDF works at federal, state, and local levels to reform policies and practices which harmfully affect large numbers of children. Activities include investigation and public information, litigation, monitoring of federal agencies, and technical assistance to local organizations. Program priorities are to assure the rights of children to proper education, adequate health care, comprehensive child care and family support services, fair and humane treatment in the juvenile justice system, and the avoidance of institutionalization.

CHILDREN'S RIGHTS
Rights of children as individuals to the protections provided in the Constitution as well as to the care and protection necessary for normal growth and development. Children's rights are actually exercised through adult representatives and advocates. The extent to which children's rights are protected varies according to the individual state laws providing for the identification and treatment of child abuse and neglect. An unresolved issue is the conflict between children's rights and parents' rights or rights to privacy. (See also PARENTS' RIGHTS)

CHIP FRACTURE (See FRACTURE)

CIRCUMSTANTIAL EVIDENCE (See EVIDENCE)

CIVIL PROCEEDING
Any lawsuit other than criminal prosecutions. Juvenile and family court cases are civil proceedings. Also called a civil action.

CLEAR AND CONVINCING EVIDENCE
(See EVIDENTIARY STANDARDS)

CLOTTING FACTOR
Material in the blood that causes it to coagulate. Deficiencies in clotting factors can cause profuse internal or external bleeding and/or bruising, as in the disease hemophilia. Bruises or bleeding caused by such a disease may be mistaken as resulting from abuse.

COLON
The large intestine.

COMMINUTED FRACTURE (See FRACTURE)

COMMISSION, ACTS OF
Overt acts by a parent or caretaker toward a child resulting in physical or mental injury, including but not limited to beatings, excessive disciplining, or exploitation. (See also CHILD ABUSE AND NEGLECT)

COMMISSIONER (See HEARING OFFICER)

COMMUNITY AWARENESS
A community's level of understanding of child abuse and neglect. Ideally, this should include knowledge about the extent and nature of the problem and how to use the local resources. In reality, community awareness tends to focus on reporting rather than treatment and prevention.

COMMUNITY COUNCIL FOR CHILD ABUSE AND NEGLECT
Community group, including both professionals and citizens, which attempts to develop and coordinate resources and/or legislation for the prevention, identification, and treatment of child abuse and neglect. It is often the name given to the program coordination component of the community team (see COMMUNITY TEAM).

COMMUNITY EDUCATION
Developed for public audiences, this type of local level education provides understanding about a problem or issue of community and/or societal relevance, and information about appropriate community resources and services available to deal with the problem or issue. Sponsored by a professional agency or citizens' group, community education is usually provided through an ongoing speaker's bureau, through periodic lecture and discussion meetings open to the general public or offered to special groups, and/or through the local media and other publicity devices.

With reference to child abuse and neglect, it is important to combine community education with public awareness. Generally, public awareness is geared only to reporting child abuse and neglect, and may communicate a punitive image toward parents who abuse or neglect their children without communicating an understanding of the problem.

COMMUNITY NEGLECT
Failure of a community to provide adequate support and social services for families and children, or lack of community control over illegal or discriminatory activities with respect to families and children.

COMMUNITY ORGANIZATION
A social work method of achieving change in human service organizations or service delivery and utilization through social planning and/or social action. This kind of intervention rests explicitly or implicitly on understanding the nature of the community or service system which is the target of change and on organizing members of the community or system to participate in the change process. Professional community organizers assist, but do not direct, community groups in developing community organization strategies of confrontation, collaboration, coalition,

etc. Since child abuse and neglect is a multidisciplinary, multiagency problem, community organization for coordination of services is imperative.

COMMUNITY SUPPORT SYSTEMS

Community resources such as schools, public health services, day care centers, welfare advocacy, whose utilization can aid in preventing family dysfunction and child abuse and neglect, and aid in treating identified cases of abuse and neglect.

COMMUNITY TEAM

Often used incorrectly to refer to a multidisciplinary professional group which only diagnoses and plans treatment for specific cases of child abuse and neglect. More accurately, a community team separates the diagnosis and treatment functions and provides a third component for education, training, and public relations. The community tream also includes a community task force or council, including citizens as well as professionals from various disciplines, which coordinates the three community team components and advocates for resources and legislation. Citizens on the community team also monitor the professionals and agency participants. For effective child abuse and neglect management, a community team should be established for every geographic area of 400,000 to 500,000 population, and should consist of the following components:

Identification/Diagnostic Team Component
The identification/diagnostic team component has primary responsibility for diagnosing actual cases of child abuse and neglect among those which are reported or otherwise come to their attention, providing acute care or crisis intervention for the child in immediate danger, and developing long-term treatment recommendations. This team should be multidisciplinary and should probably include a public health nurse, pediatrician, psychologist or psychiatrist, lawyer, law enforcement person, case aides, and a number of child protective services workers. The protective services workers on the diagnostic team undergo unusual physical and emotional fatigue, and they should have a two or three week break from this activity every several months. However, to further relieve this stress, the diagnostic team, and not the protective services workers alone, should make and be accountable for all decisions. To function effectively, this team must establish protocol, define roles of each team member, establish policies and procedures, and establish a network of coordination with acute care service agencies.

Long Term Treatment Component
The long term treatment component has responsibility to review treatment needs and progress of specific cases periodically, to establish treatment goals, to coordinate existing treatment services, and to develop new treatment programs. This component should include supervisors and workers from supportive and advocacy services as well as from adult, children, and family treatment programs. The community team must assure provision and use of this component.

Education, Training, and Public Relations Component
The education, training, and public relations component has responsibility for community and professional awareness and education. Professional education includes implementation and/or evaluation of ongoing training programs for professionals and paraprofessionals.

The interrelationship among these various components is diagrammed below:

A - Identification and Diagnosis	1 - Case Coordination
B - Long-Term Treatment	2 - Professional Training and Recruitment
C - Education, Training, Public Relations	3 - Public and Professional ducation, Professional Training
	4 - Program Coordination

COMPLIANCE
1) The behavior of children who readily yield to demands in an attempt to please abusive or neglectful parents or caretakers.
2) A state child abuse and neglect law which conforms to requirements outlined in the Child Abuse Prevention and Treatment Act and further HEW regulations, and which therefore permits funding under this act for child abuse and neglect activities in the state. (See also CHILD ABUSE PREVENTION AND TREATMENT ACT)

COMPLAINT
1) An oral statement, usually made to the police, charging criminal, abusive, or neglectful conduct.
2) A district attorney's document which starts a criminal prosecution.
3) A petitioner's document which starts a civil proceeding. In juvenile or family court, the complaint is usually called a petition.
4) In some states, term used for a report of suspected abuse or neglect.

COMPOUND FRACTURE (See FRACTURE)

COMPREHENSIVE EMERGENCY SERVICES(CES)
A community system of coordinated services available on a 24-hour basis to meet emergency needs of children and/or families in crisis. Components of a CES system can include 24-hour protective services, homemaker services, crisis nurseries, family shelters, emergency foster care, outreach, and follow-up services.

CONCILIATION COURT (See COURTS)

CONCUSSION
An injury of a soft structure resulting from violent shaking or jarring; usually refers to a brain concussion.

CONFIDENTIALITY
Professional practice of not sharing with others information entrusted by a client or patient. Sometimes communications from parent to physician or social worker are made with this expectation but are later used in court, and many physicians and social workers are torn between legal vs. professional obligations. Confidentiality which is protected by statute is known as privileged communications. Confidentiality need not obstruct information sharing with a multidisciplinary team provided that the client is advised of the sharing and the team has articulated its own policy and guidelines on confidentiality. (See also PRIVILEGED COMMUNICATIONS)

CONGENITAL
Refers to any physical condition present at birth, regardless of its cause.

CONJUNCTIVA
Transparent lining covering the white of the eye and eyelids. Bleeding beneath the conjunctiva can occur spontaneously or from accidental or non-accidental injury.

CONTRAINDICATION
Reason for not giving a particular drug or prescribing a particular treatment, as it may do more harm than good.

CONTUSION
A wound producing injury to soft tissue without a break in the skin, causing bleeding into surrounding tissues.

CORPORAL PUNISHMENT
Physical punishment inflicted directly upon the body. Some abusive parents mistakenly believe that corporal punishment is the only way to discipline children, and some child development specialists believe that almost all parents must occasionally resort to corporal punishment to discipline or train children. Other professionals believe that corporal punishment is never advisable. In a Supreme Court ruling (Ingraham vs. Wright, April 19, 1977), corporal punishment in the schools was upheld. The Supreme Court ruled that the cruel and unusual punishment clause of the Eighth Amendment does not apply to corporal punishment in the schools. (See also DISCIPLINE).

CORTEX
Outer layer of an organ or other body structure.

COURTS
Places where judicial proceedings occur. There is an array of courts involved with child abuse and neglect cases, partly because different states divide responsibility for certain proceedings among different courts, and also because tradition has established a variety of names for courts which perform similar functions. Child abuse reports can result in proceedings in any of the following courts:

Criminal Court
Usually divided into superior court, which handles felony cases, and municipal court, which handles misdemeanors and the beginning stages of most felony cases.

Domestic Relations Court
A civil court in which divorces and divorce custody hearings are held.

Family Court
A civil court which, in some states, combines the functions of domestic relations, juvenile, and probate courts. Establishment of family courts is often urged to reform the presently wasteful and poorly-coordinated civil court system. Under some proposals, family courts would also deal with criminal cases involving family relations, thus improving coordination in child abuse litigation.

Court of Conciliation
A branch of domestic relations courts in some states, usually staffed by counselors and social workers rather than by lawyers or judges, and designed to explore and promote reconciliation in divorce cases.

Juvenile Court
Juvenile court, which has jurisdiction over minors, usually handles cases of suspected delinquency as well as cases of suspected abuse or neglect. In many states, terminations of parental rights occur in juvenile court proceedings, but that is generally the limit of juvenile court's power over adults.

Probate Court
Probate court may handle cases of guardianship and adoption in addition to estates of deceased persons.

CRANIUM
The skull.

CRIMINAL PROSECUTION
The process involving the filing of charges of a crime, followed by arraignment and trial of the defendant. Criminal prosecution may result in fines, imprisonment, and/or probation. Criminal defendants are entitled to acquittal unless charges against them are proven beyond a reasonable doubt. Technical rules of evidence exclude many kinds of proof in criminal trials, even though that proof might be admissible in civil proceedings. Criminal defendants are entitled to a jury trial; in many civil proceedings concerning children, there is no right to a jury trial.

CRISIS INTERVENTION
Action to relieve a specific stressful situation or series of problems which are immediately threatening to a child's health and/or welfare. This involves alleviation of parental stress through provision of emergency services in the home and/or removal of the child from the home. (See also EMERGENCY SERVICES and COMPREHENSIVE EMERGENCY SERVICES)

CRISIS NURSERY
Facility offering short-term relief of several hours to several days' duration to parents temporarily unable or unwilling to care for their children. The primary purpose are child protection, stabilization of the home, and prevention of child abuse and neglect.

CUSTODY
The right to care and control of a child and the duty to provide food, clothing, shelter, ordinary medical care, education, and discipline for a child. Permanent legal custody

may be taken from a parent or given up by a parent by a court action (see TERMINATION OF PARENTAL RIGHTS). Temporary custody of a child may be granted for a limited time only, usually pending further action or review by the court. Temporary custody may be granted for a period of months or, in the case of protective or emergency custody, for a period of hours or several days.

Emergency Custody
The ability of a law enforcement officer, pursuant to the criminal code, to take temporary custody of a child who is in immediate danger and place him/her in the control of child protective services. A custody hearing must usually be held within 48 hours of such action. Also known as police custody.

Protective Custody
Emergency measure taken to detain a child, often in a hospital, until a written detention request can be filed. In some states, telephone communication with a judge is required to authorize protective custody. In other states, police, social workers, or doctors have statutory authority to detain minors who are in imminent danger. (See also DETENTION)

CUSTODY HEARING
Hearing, usually held in children's court, to determine who has the rights of legal custody of a minor. It may involve one parent against the other or the parents vs. a social service agency.

CYCLE OF CHILD ABUSE OR NEGLECT
(See WORLD OF ABNORMAL REARING)

DAUGHTERS UNITED
Organization name sometimes used for self-help groups of daughters who have been sexually abused. Daughters United is one component of a model Child Sexual Abuse Treatment Program in Santa Clara County, California. (See also PARENTS UNITED)

DAY CARE
A structured, supervised place for children to go more or less regularly while parents work or attend school. Experts believe that family stress can be relieved by more extensive provision of day care services, and day care providers are increasingly concerned with identification and prevention of child abuse and neglect.

DAY TREATMENT
1) Program providing treatment as well as structured supervision for children with identified behavioral problems, including abused and neglected children, while they remain in their own, foster, or group homes. Day treatment services usually include counseling with families or caretakers with whom the children reside.
2) Treatment and structured activities for parents or entire families in a treatment setting from which they return to their own homes evenings and weekends.

DELINQUENCY
Behavior of a minor which would, in the case of an adult, constitute criminal conduct. In some states, delinquency also includes "waywardness" or disobedient behavior on the part of the child. In contrast to dependency cases, where the parent(s) rather than the minor is assumed responsible, delinquency cases assume that the minor has some responsibility for his/her behavior.

DENVER MODEL
A multidisciplinary hospital-community coalition which originated in Denver, Colorado, and which has become a model replicated by many other programs. The following diagram outlines the components:

TIME	PLACE	FUNCTION
	Community	Child is identified as suspected abuse or neglect.
24 hours	Hospital	Child is admitted to hospital.
	Hospital	Telephone report is made to protective services.
	Community	Home is evaluated by protective services.
72 hours	Both	Dispositional conference is held.
	Community	Court is involved if needed.
2 weeks	Both	Implement dispositional plan.
6-9 months	Community	Maintain case.
	Both	Long-term Treatment program is followed.
	Both	Child is returned home when home has been made safe.

DEPENDENCY

A child's need for care and supervision from a parent or caretaker. Often a legal term referring to cases of children whose natural parent(s) cannot or will not properly care for them or supervise them so that the state must assume this responsibility. Many states distinguish findings of dependency, for which the juvenile is assumed to have little or no responsibility, from findings of delinquency, in which the juvenile is deemed to be at least partially responsible for his/her behavior.

DETENTION

The temporary confinement of a person by a public authority. In a case of child abuse or neglect, a child may be detained pending a trial when a detention hearing indicates that it is unsafe for the child to remain in his/her own home. This is often called protective custody or emergency custody. The child may be detained in a foster home, group home, hospital, or other facility.

DETENTION HEARING

A court hearing held to determine whether a child should be kept away from his/her parents until a full trial of neglect, abuse, or delinquency allegations can take place. Detention hearings must usually be held within 24 hours of the filing of a detention request. (See also CUSTODY)

DETENTION REQUEST

A document filed by a probation officer, social worker, or prosecutor with the clerk of a juvenile or family court, asking that a detention hearing be held, and that a child be detained until the detention hearing has taken place. Detention requests must usually be filed within 48 hours of the time protective custody of the child begins. (See also CUSTODY)

DIAGNOSTIC TEAM (See COMMUNITY TEAM)

DIAPHYSIS

The shaft of a long bone.

DIFFERENTIAL DIAGNOSIS

The determination of which of two or more diseases or conditions a patient may be suffering from by systematically comparing and contrasting the clinical findings.

DIRECT EVIDENCE (See EVIDENCE)

DIRECT SERVICE PROVIDERS

Those groups and individuals who directly interact with clients and patients in the delivery of health, education, and welfare services, or those agencies which employs them. It includes, among others, policemen, social workers, physicians, psychiatrists, and clinical psychologists who see clients or patients.

DISCIPLINE

1) A branch of knowledge or learning or a particular profession, such as law, medicine, or social work.
2) Training that develops self-control, self-sufficiency, orderly conduct. Discipline is

often confused with punishment, particularly by abusive parents who resort to corporal punishment. Although interpretations of both "discipline" and "punishment" tend to be vague and often overlapping, there is some consensus that discipline has positive connotations and punishment is considered negatively. Some general comparisons between the terms are:
a) Discipline can occur before, during, and/or after an event; punishment occurs only after an event.
b) Discipline is based on respect for a child and his/her capabilities; punishment is based on behavior or events precipitating behavior.
c) Discipline implies that there is an authority figure; punishment implies power and dominance vs. submissiveness.
d) The purpose of discipline is educational and rational; the purpose of punishment is to inflict pain, often in an attempt to vent frustration or anger.
e) Discipline focuses on deterring future behavior by encouraging development of internal controls; punishment is a method of external control which may or may not alter future behavior.
f) Discipline can lead to extrapolation and generalized learning patterns; punishment may relate only to a specific event.
g) Discipline can strengthen interpersonal bonds and recognizes individual means and worth; punishment usually causes deterioration of relationships and is usually a dehumanizing experience.
h) Both discipline and punishment behavior patterns may be transmitted to the next generation.

According to legal definitions applying to most schools and school districts, to accomplish the purposes of education, a schoolteacher stands in the place of a parent and may exercise powers of control, restraint, discipline, and correction as necessary, provided that the discipline is reasonable. The Supreme Court has ruled that under certain circumstances, the schools may also employ corporal punishment. (See also CORPORAL PUNISHMENT)

DISLOCATION
The displacement of a bone, usually disrupting a joint, which may accompany a fracture or may occur alone.

DISPOSITION
The order of a juvenile or family court issued at a dispositional hearing which determines whether a minor, already found to be a dependent or delinquent child, should continue in or return to the parental home, and under what kind of supervision, or whether the minor should be placed out-of-home, and in what kind of setting: a relative's home, foster home, or institution. Disposition in a civil case parallels sentencing in a criminal case.

DISPOSITIONAL CONFERENCE
A conference, preferably multidisciplinary, in which the child, parent, family, and home diagnostic assessments are evaluated and decisions are made as to court involvement, steps needed to protect the child, and type of long-term treatment. This conference should be held within the first 72 hours after hospital admission or reporting of the case.

DISPOSITIONAL HEARING (See DISPOSITION)

DISTAL
Far; farther from any point of reference. Opposite of proximal.

DOMESTIC RELATIONS COURT (See COURTS)

DUE PROCESS
The rights of persons involved in legal proceedings to be treated with fairness. These rights include the right to adequate notice in advance of hearings, the right to notice of allegations of misconduct, the right to assis-

tance of a lawyer, the right to confront and cross-examine witnesses, and the right to refuse to give self-incriminating testimony. In child abuse or neglect cases, courts are granting more and more due process to parents in recognition of the fact that loss of parental rights, temporarily or permanently, is as serious as loss of liberty. However, jury trials and presumptions of innocence are still afforded in very few juvenile or family court cases.

DUODENUM
The first portion of the small intestine which connects it to the stomach.

EARLY AND PERIODIC SCREENING, DIAGNOSIS, AND TREATMENT (EPSDT)
Program enacted in 1967 under Medicaid (Title 19 of the Social Security Act), with early detection of potentially crippling or disabling conditions among poor children as its goal. The establishment of EPSDT was a result of studies indicating that physical and mental defects were high among poor children and that early detection of the problems and prompt receipt of health care could reduce the consequences and the need for remedial services in later life. Although a recent study by the Children's Defense Fund has indicated that existing health systems are not adequate to facilitate the goals of EPSDT, the program has uncovered many previously undetected or untreated health problems among those children whom it has been able to reach.

EARLY INTERVENTION
Programs and services focusing on prevention by relieving family stress before child abuse and neglect occur; for example, helplines, Head Start, home health visitors, EPSDT, crisis nurseries.

ECCHYMOSIS (See INTRADERMAL HEMORRHAGE)

EDEMA
Swelling caused by an excessive amount of fluid in body tissue. It often follows a bump or bruise but may also be caused by allergy, malnutrition, or disease.

EMERGENCY CUSTODY (See CUSTODY)

EMERGENCY SERVICES
The focus of these services is protection of a child and prevention of further maltreatment through availability of a reporting mechanism on a 24-hour basis and immediate intervention. This intervention could include hospitalization of the child, assistance in the home including homemakers, or removal of the child from the home to a shelter or foster home. (See also COMPREHENSIVE EMERGENCY SERVICES)

EMOTIONAL ABUSE (See CHILD ABUSE AND NEGLECT)

EMOTIONAL NEGLECT (See CHILD ABUSE AND NEGLECT)

ENCOPRESIS
Involuntary passage of feces.

ENURESIS
Involuntary passage of urine.

EPIPHYSIS
Growth center near the end of a long bone.

EVIDENCE
Any sort of proof submitted to the court for the purpose of influencing the court's decision. Some special kinds of evidence are:

Circumstantial
Proof of circumstances which may imply another fact. For example, proof that a parent kept a broken appliance cord may connect the parent to infliction of unique marks on a child's body.

Direct
Generally consisting of testimony of the type such as a neighbor stating that he/she saw the parent strike the child with an appliance cord.

Hearsay
Second-hand evidence, generally consisting of testimony of the type such as, "I heard him say. . . ." Except in certain cases, such evidence is usually excluded because it is considered unreliable and because the person making the original statement cannot be cross-examined.

Opinion
Although witnesses are ordinarily not permitted to testify to their beliefs or opinions, being restricted instead to reporting what they actually saw or heard, when a witness can be qualified as an expert on a given subject, he/she can report his/her conclusions, for example, "Based upon these marks, it is my opinion as a doctor that the child must have been struck with a flexible instrument very much like this appliance cord." Lawyers are sometimes allowed to ask qualified experts "hypothetical questions," in which the witness is asked to assume the truth of certain facts and to express an opinion based on those "facts." (See also EXPERT TESTIMONY)

Physical
Any tangible piece of proof such as a document, X-ray, photograph, or weapon used to inflict an injury. Physical evidence must usually be authenticated by a witness who testifies to the connection of the evidence (also called an exhibit) with other facts in the case.

Evidentiary Standards
State laws differ in the quantum of evidence which is considered necessary to prove a case of child maltreatment. Three of the most commonly used standards are:

Beyond a Reasonable Doubt (the standard required in all criminal court proceedings). Evidence which is entirely convincing or satisfying to a moral certainty. This is the strictest standard of all.

Clear and Convincing Evidence. Less evidence than is required to prove a case beyond a reasonable doubt, but still an amount which would make one confident of the truth of the allegations.

Preponderance of the Evident (the standard in most civil court proceedings). Merely presenting a greater weight of credible evidence than that presented by the opposing party. This is the easiest standard of proof of all.

EXHIBIT
Physical evidence used in court. In a child abuse case, an exhibit may consist of X-rays, photographs of the child's injuries, or the actual materials presumably used to inflict the injuries. (See also EVIDENCE)

EXPERT TESTIMONY
Witnesses with various types of expertise may testify in child abuse or neglect cases; usually these expert witnesses are physicians or radiologists. Experts are usually questioned in court about their education or experience which qualifies them to give professional opinions about the matter in question. Only after the hearing officer determines that the witness is, in fact, sufficiently expert in the subject matter may that witness proceed to state his/her opinions. (See also EVIDENCE)

EXPERT WITNESS (See EXPERT TESTIMONY)

EXPLOITATION OF CHILDREN
1) Involving a child in illegal or immoral activities for the benefit of a parent or caretaker. This could include child pornography, child prostitution, sexual abuse, or forcing a child to steal.
2) Forcing workloads on a child in or outside the home so as to interfere with the health, education, and well-being of the child.

EXPUNGEMENT

Destruction of records. Expungement may be ordered by the court after a specified number of years or when the juvenile, parent, or defendant applies for expungement and shows that his/her conduct has improved. Expungement also applies to the removal of an unverified report of abuse or neglect that has been made to a central registry. (See also CENTRAL REGISTRY)

EXTRAVASATED BLOOD
Discharge or escape of blood into tissue.

FAILURE TO THRIVE SYNDROME (FTT)
A serious medical condition most often seen in children under one year of age. An FTT child's height, weight, and motor development fall significantly short of the average growth rates of normal children. In about 10% of FTT cases, there is an organic cause such as serious heart, kidney, or intestinal disease, a genetic error of metabolisin, or brain damage. All other cases are a result of a disturbed parent-child relationship manifested in severe physical and emotional neglect of the child. In diagnosing FTT as child neglect, certain criteria should be considered:
1) The child's weight is below the third percentile, but substantial weight gain occurs when the child is properly nurtured, such as when hospitalized.
2) The child exhibits developmental retardation which decreases when there is adequate feeding and appropriate stimulation.
3) Medical investigation provides no evidence that disease or medical abnormality is causing the symptoms.
4) The child exhibits clinical signs of deprivation which decrease in a more nurturing environment.
5) There appears to be a significant environmental psychosocial disruption in the child's family.

FAMILIES ANONYMOUS
1) Name used by the National Center for the Prevention and Treatment of Child Abuse and Neglect at Denver for self-help groups for abusive parents. These groups operate in much the same way as the more widely-known Parents Anonymous. (See also PARENTS ANONYMOUS)
2) Self-help groups for families of drug abusers.

FAMILIES-AT-RISK
May refer to families evidencing high potential for child abuse or neglect because of a conspicuous, severe parental problem, such as criminal behavior, substance abuse, mental retardation, or psychosis. More often refers to families evidencing high potential for abuse or neglect because of risk factors which may be less conspicuous but multiple. These include: 1) environmental stress such as unemployment or work dissatisfaction; social isolation; anomie; lack of child care resources; I and/or 2) family stress such as marital discord; chronically and/or emotionally immature parent with a history of abuse or neglect as a child; unwanted pregnancy; colicky, hyperactive, or handicapped baby or child; siblings a year or less apart; sudden changes in family due to illness, separation, or death; parentla ignorance of child care and child development. Increasingly, the maternal-infant bonding process at childbirth is evaluated and used as one means to identify families-at-risk. Families thus identified should be offered immediate and periodic assistance.

FAMILY
Two or more persons related by blood, marriage, or mutual agreement who interact and provide one another with mutual physical, emotional, social, and/or economic care. Families can be described as "extended," with more than one generation in a household; or "nuclear," with only parent(s) and child(ren). Families can also be described as "mixed" or "multiracial"; "multi-parent," as in a commune or collective; or "single-parent." These types are not mutually exclusive.

FAMILY COURT (See COURTS)

FAMILY DYNAMICS
Interrelationships between and among individual family members. The evaluation of family dynamics is an important factor in the

identification, diagnosis, and treatment of child abuse and neglect.

FAMILY DYSFUNCTION
Ineffective functioning of the family as a unit or of individual family members in their family role because of physical, mental, or situational problems of one or more family members. A family which does not have or use internal or external resources to cope with its problems or fulfill its responsibilities to children may be described as dysfunctional. Child abuse and neglect is evidence of family dysfunction.

FAMILY IMPACT STATEMENT
Report which assesses the effect of existing and proposed legislation, policies, regulations, and practices on family life. The purpose is to promote legislation and policies which work for, not against, healthy family life. At the federal level, this activity is being developed by the Family Impact Seminar, George Washington University Institute for Educational Leadership (1001 Connecticut Ave., N.W., Suite 732, Washington, D.C. 20036).

FAMILY LIFE EDUCATION
Programs focusing on educating, enlightening, and supporting individuals and families regarding aspects of family life; for example, child development classes, communication skills workshops, sex education courses, or money management courses. Family life education might well be part of every child abuse and neglect prevention program, and may be part of the treatment program for abusive or neglectful parents who lack this information.

FAMILY PLANNING
Information and counseling provided to assist in controlling family size and spacing of children, including referrals to various agencies such as Planned Parenthood.

As a condition of receiving federal funding for AFDC (see SOCIAL SECURITY ACT), states are required to offer family planning services to applicants designated as "appropriate."

Family planning should be part of a child abuse and neglect prevention program.

FAMILY POLICY
Generally refers to public social and economic policies that centrally affect families. There is considerable confusion about the term, with some persons believing that family policy should mean more direct policies affecting families, such as family planning policies. There is much more agreement that we should look at the impact of numerous policies on families, and that these should include a wide range of governmental policies. (See also FAMILY IMPACT STATEMENT)

FAMILY SHELTER
A 24-hour residential care facility for entire families. The setting offers around-the-clock care, and often provides diagnosis and comprehensive treatment on a short-term basis. In child abuse and neglect, a family shelter is used primarily for crisis intervention.

FAMILY SYSTEM
The concept that families operate as an interacting whole and are an open system, so that many factors in the environment affect the functioning of family members and the interaction among members. It is also conceptualized that the behavior of the family as an interacting unit has an effect on a number of factors in the outer environment.

FAMILY VIOLENCE
Abusive or aggressive behavior between parents, known as wife battering or spouse abuse; between children, known as sibling abuse; and/or between parents and children within a family, usually child abuse. This behavior is related to factors within the structure of a family system and/or society; for example, poverty, models of violent behavior displayed via mass media, stress due to excessive numbers of children, values of dominance and submissiveness, and attitudes toward discipline and punishment. It may also occur as a result of alcoholism or other substance abuse.

The terms family violence and domestic violence are sometimes used interchangeably but some persons exclude child abuse from the definition of domestic violence and limit it to violence between adult mates or spouses.

FEDERAL REGULATIONS
Guidelines and regulations developed by departments or agencies of the federal government to govern programs administered or funded by those agencies. Regulations specify policies and procedures outlined in a more general way in public laws or acts. Proposed federal regulations, or changes in existing regulations, are usually published in the *Federal Register* for public review and comment. They are subsequently published in the final form adopted by the governing agency.

FEDERAL STANDARDS (See STANDARDS)

FELONY
A serious crime for which the punishment may be imprisonment for longer than a year and/or a fine greater than $1,000. Distinguished from misdemeanor or infraction, both of lesser degree.

FIFTH AMENDMENT
The Fifth Amendment to the U.S. Constitution guarantees a defendant that he/she cannot be compelled to present self-incriminating testimony.

FONTANEL
The soft spots on a baby's skull where the bones of the skull have not yet grown together.

FORENSIC MEDICINE
That branch of the medical profession concerned with establishing evidence for legal proceedings.

FOSTER CARE
A form of substitute care for children who need to be removed from their own homes. Usually this is a temporary placement in which a child lives with a licensed foster family or caretaker until he/she can return to his/her own home or until reaching the age of majority. Foster care all too often becomes a permanent method of treatment for abused or neglected children. Effective foster care ideally includes service to the child, service to the natural parents, service to the foster parents, and periodic review of the placement.

FOSTER GRANDPARENTS
Retired persons or senior citizens who provide nurturance and support for children to whom they are not related, including abused and neglected children, by babysitting or taking them for recreational outings. This enables parents to have some respite and allows retired or older persons an opportunity to become involved in community activities. Sometimes foster grandparents are volunteers and sometimes they are paid by an agency program.

FOUNDED REPORT
Any report of suspected child abuse or neglect made to the mandated agency which is confirmed or verified. Founded reports outnumber unfounded reports.

FRACTURE
A broken bone, which is one of the most common injuries found among battered children. The fracture may occur in several ways:

Chip Fracture
A small piece of bone is flaked from the major part of the bone.

Comminuted Fracture
Bone is crushed or broken into a number of pieces.

Compound Fracture
Fragment(s) of broken bone protrudes through the skin, causing a wound.

Simple Fracture
Bone breaks without wounding the surrounding tissue.

Spiral Fracture

Twisting causes the line of the fracture to encircle the bone like a spiral staircase.

Torus Fracture
A folding, bulging, or buckling fracture. See diagram on next page for names and locations of the major bones of the human skeleton.

FRONTAL
Referring to the front of the head; the forehead.

FUNDASCOPIC EXAM
Opthalmic examination to determine if irregularities or internal injuries to the eye exist.

GATEKEEPERS
Professionals and the agencies which employ them who are in frequent or periodic contact with families or children and who are therefore in an advantageous position to spot individual and family problems, including child abuse and neglect, and make appropriate referrals for early intervention or treatment.

GLUTEAL
Related to the buttocks, which are made up of the large gluteus maximus muscles.

GONORRHEA (See VENEREAL DISEASE)

GRAND ROUNDS
Hospital staff meetings for presentation and discussion of a particular case or medical problem.

GUARDIAN
Adult charged lawfully with the responsibility for a child. A guardian has almost all the rights and powers of a natural parent, but the relationship is subject to termination or change. A guardian may or may not also have custody and therefore actual care and supervision of the child.

GUARDIAN AD LITEM (GAL)
Adult appointed by the court to represent the child in a judicial proceeding. The *guardian ad litem* may be, but is not necessarily, an attorney. Under the Child Abuse Prevention and Treatment Act, a state cannot qualify for federal assistance unless it provides by statute "that in every case involving an abused or neglected child which results in a judicial proceeding a *guardian ad litem* shall be appointed to represent the child in such proceedings." Some states have begun to allow a GAL for children in divorce cases.

HEAD START
A nationwide comprehensive program for disadvantaged preschool children, funded by the HEW Administration for Children, Youth and Families to meet the educational, nutritional, and health needs of the children and to encourage parent participation in their children's development.

Through federal policy instructions (see *Federal Register,* January 26, 1977), all Head Start staff are mandated to report suspected cases of child abuse and neglect. These policy instructions supersede individual child abuse and neglect reporting laws in states which do not include Head Start staff as mandated reporters.

HEARING
Judicial proceeding where issues of fact or law are tried and in which both parties have a right to be heard. A hearing is synonymous with a trial.

HEARING OFFICER
A judge or other individual who presides at a judicial proceeding. The role of judge is performed in some juvenile court hearings by referees or commissioners, whose orders are issued in the name of the supervising judge. Acts of a referee or commissioner may be undone after the supervising judge has conducted a rehearing in the case.

HELPLINE
Usually a telephone counseling, information, and referral service characterized by caller anonymity, late hour availability, and the use

of trained volunteers as staff. The goal is usually early intervention in any kind of family stress, as well as crisis intervention in child abuse and neglect. Helplines relieve social isolation and offer ways of ventilating stress which are not destructive. Unlike hotlines, helplines generally cannot report cases of child abuse and neglect since they do not know the caller's name. Instead, the helpline attempts to have the caller himself/herself seek professional assistance and/or maintain a regular calling relationship for support and as an alternative to violent behavior. Helplines appear to be very cost effective in the preventive of child abuse and neglect. Major disadvantages are lack of visual cues to problems and limited opportunity for follow-up services. (See also HOTLINE)

HEMATEMESIS
Vomiting of blood from the stomach, often resulting from internal injuries.

HEMATOMA
A swelling caused by a collection of blood in an enclosed space, such as under the skin or the skull.

HEMATUREA
Blood in the urine.

HEMOPHILIA
Hereditary blood clotting disorder characterized by spontaneous or traumatic internal and external bleeding and bruising.

HEMOPTYSIS
Spitting or coughing blood from the windpipe or lungs.

HEMORRHAGE
The escape of blood from the vessels; bleeding.

HOME HEALTH VISITOR (See CHILD HEALTH VISITOR)

HOME START
A nationwide home-based program funded by the HEW Administration for Children, Youth and Families to strengthen parents as educators of their own children.

HOMEMAKER SERVICES
Provision of assistance, support, and relief for parents who may be unable or unwilling to fulfill parenting functions because of illness or being overwhelmed with parenting responsibilities. A homemaker is placed in a home on an hourly or weekly basis and assists with housekeeping and child care while demonstrating parenting skills and providing some degree of nurturance for parents and children.

HOSPITAL HOLD
Hospitalization for further observation and protection of a child suspected of being abused or neglected. This usually occurs when a suspected case is discovered in an emergency room. In most cases, holding the child is against the wishes of the parent or caretaker. (See also CUSTODY)

HOTLINE
Twenty-four hour statewide or local answering service for reporting child abuse or neglect and initiating investigation by a local agency. This is often confused with a helpline. (See also HELPLINE)

HYPERACTIVE
More active than is considered normal.

HYPERTHERMIA
Condition of high body temperature.

HYPHEMA
Hemorrhage within the anterior chamber of the eye, often appearing as a bloodshot eye. The cause could be a blow to the head or violent shaking.

HYPOACTIVE
Less active than is considered normal.

HYPOTHERMIA
Condition of low body temperature.

HYPOVITAMINOSIS

Condition due to the deficiency of one or more essential vitamins. (See also AVITAMINOSIS)

IDENTIFICATION OF CHILD ABUSE AND NEGLECT

Diagnosis or verification of child abuse and neglect cases by mandated agency workers or a diagnostic team following investigation of suspected child abuse and neglect (see INDICATORS OF CHILD ABUSE AND NEGLECT). Identification of child abuse and neglect therefore depends not only on professional diagnostic skill but also on the extent to which the public and professionals report suspected cases. Public awareness campaigns are important to effect identification, but at the same time it is important to have sufficient staff in the mandated agency to handle all the reports a public awareness campaign may generate (see COMMUNITY AWARENESS and COMMUNITY EDUCATION). More reporting and therefore identification will also occur as states strengthen their reporting laws so as to extend the number of persons who must report and penalize them more heavily if they don't. It is generally agreed that to date the identification of child abuse and neglect represents only a small proportion of the actual incidence of the problem. It is also generally agreed that a greater degree of identification occurs in minority and low income groups because these persons are more visible to agencies and professionals required to report. The incidence is probably as high in upper socio-economic groups, but identification is more difficult, particularly because private physicians generally dislike to report.

ILEUM

Final portion of the small intestine which connects with the colon.

IMMUNITY, LEGAL

Legal protection from civil or criminal liability.
1) Child abuse and neglect reporting statutes often confer immunity upon persons mandated to report, giving them an absolute defense to libel, slander, invasion of privacy, false arrest, and other lawsuits which the person accused of the act might file. Some grants of immunity are limited only to those persons who report in good faith and without malicious intent.
2) Immunity from criminal liability is sometimes conferred upon a witness in order to obtain vital testimony. Thereafter, the witness cannot be prosecuted with the use of information he/she disclosed in his/her testimony. If an immunized witness refuses to testify, he/she can be imprisoned for contempt of court.

IMPETIGO

A highly contagious, rapidly spreading skin disorder which occurs principally in infants and young children. The disease, characterized by red blisters, may be an indicator of neglect and poor living conditions.

IMPULSE-RIDDEN MOTHER

Term often used to describe one kind of neglectful parent who demonstrates restlessness, aggressiveness, inability to tolerate stress, manipulativeness, and craving for excitement or change. This parent may have a lesser degree of early deprivation than the apathetic-futile parent, but lacks self-control over strong impulses and/or has not learned limit-setting.

IN CAMERA

Any closed hearing before a judge in his chambers is said to be *in camera*.

IN LOCO PARENTIS

"In the place of a parent." Refers to actions of a guardian or other non-parental custodian.

INCEST

Sexual intercourse between persons who are closely related. Some state laws recognize incest only as sexual intercourse among consaguineous, or blood, relations; other states recognize incest as sexual relations between a variety of family members related by blood and/or law. In the U.S., the prohibition against incest is specified by many states' laws as well as by cultural tradition, with state laws usually defining incest as marriage or sexual relationships between relatives who are closer than second, or sometimes even more distant, cousins. While incest and sexual abuse are sometimes thought to be synonymous, it should be realized that incest is only one aspect of sexual abuse. Incest can occur within families between members of the same sex, but the most common form of incest is between father and daughters. It is generally agreed that incest is much more common than the number of reported cases indicates. Also, because society has not until the present done much about this problem, professionals have generally not had adequate training to deal with it, and the way the problem is handled may prove more traumatic for a child victim of incest than the incest experience itself. It should be noted that sexual relations between relatives may be defined as incest, but that in cest is not considered child sexual abuse unless a minor is involved. (See also CHILD ABUSE AND NEGLECT, SEXUAL ABUSE, SEXUAL MISUSE)

INCIDENCE
The extent to which a problem occurs in a given population. No accurate or complete data is available on the actual incidence of child abuse and neglect in the U.S. because major studies have not been able to obtain data from some states or have found the data not to be comparable. For continuing efforts to solve this problem, see NATIONAL STUDY ON CHILD ABUSE AND NEGLECT REPORTING. Informed estimates of incidence range from 600,000 to one million cases of child abuse and neglect per year in this country. It is generally agreed that child neglect is four to five or more times more common than child abuse. Incidence of actual child abuse and neglect should not be confused with the number of reported cases in a central registry, since the latter include reports of suspected but unconfirmed cases. On the other hand, it is generally agreed that because of insufficient reporting, the number of actual cases coming to the attention of local agencies is but a small proportion of the actual number of cases in the population. (See also CENTRAL REGISTRY and IDENTIFICATION OF CHILD ABUSE AND NEGLECT)

INDICATED CHILD ABUSE AND NEGLECT
1) In some state statutes, "indicated" child abuse and neglect means a confirmed or verified case.
2) Medically, "indicated" means a probable case.

INDICATORS OF CHILD ABUSE AND NEGLECT
Signs or symptoms which, when found in various combinations, point to possible abuse or neglect. See chart on next page for common indicators of child abuse and neglect.

INDICTMENT
The report of a grand jury charging an adult with criminal conduct. The process of indictment by secret grand jury proceedings bypasses the filing of a criminal complaint and the holding of a preliminary hearing in municipal court, so that prosecution begins immediately in superior court.

INFANTICIDE
The killing of an infant or many infants. Until modern times, infanticide was an accepted method of population control. It often took the form of abandonment. A few primitive cultures still practice infanticide.

Indicators of Child Abuse and Neglect

CATEGORY	CHILD'S APPEARANCE	CHILD'S BEHAVIOR	CARETAKER'S BEHAVIOR
Physical Abuse	—Bruises and welts (on the face, lips, or mouth; in various stages of healing; on large areas of the torso, back, buttocks, or thighs; in unusual patterns, clustered, or reflective of the instrument used to inflict them; on several different surface areas). —Burns (cigar or cigarette burns; glove or sock-like burns or doughnut shaped burns on the buttocks or genitalia indicative of immersion in hot liquid; rope burns on the arms, legs, neck or torso; patterned burns that show the shape of the item (iron, grill, etc.) used to inflict them). —Fractures (skull, jaw, or nasal fractures; spiral fractures of the long (arm and leg) bones; fractures in various states of healing; multiple fractures; any fracture in a child under the age of two). —Lacerations and abrasions (to the mouth, lip, gums, or eye; to the external genitalia). —Human bite marks.	—Wary of physical contact with adults. —Apprehensive when other children cry. —Demonstrates extremes in behavior (e.g., extreme aggressiveness or withdrawal). —Seems frightened of parents. —Reports injury by parents.	—Has history of abuse as a child. —Uses harsh discipline inappropriate to child's age, transgression, and condition. —Offers illogical, unconvincing, contradictory, or no explanation of child's injury. —Seems unconcerned about child. —Significantly misperceives child (e.g., sees him as bad, evil, a monster, etc.). —Psychotic or psychopathic. —Misuses alcohol or other drugs. —Attempts to conceal child's injury or to protect identity of person responsible.
Neglect	—Consistently dirty, unwashed, hungry, or inappropriately dressed. —Without supervision for extended periods of time or when engaged in dangerous activities. —Constantly tired or listless. —Has unattended physical problems or lacks routine medical care. —Is exploited, overworked, or kept from attending school. —Has been abandoned.	—Is engaging in delinquent acts (e.g., vandalism, drinking, prostitution, drug use, etc.) —Is begging or stealing food. —Rarely attends school.	—Misuses alcohol or other drugs. —Maintains chaotic home life. —Shows evidence of apathy or futility. —Is mentally ill or of diminished intelligence. —Has long-term chronic illnesses. —Has history of neglect as a child.
Sexual Abuse	—Has torn, stained, or bloody underclothing. —Experience pain or itching in the genital area. —Has bruises or bleeding in external genitalia, vagina, or anal regions. —Has venereal disease. —Has swollen or red cervix, vulva, or perineum. —Has semen around mouth or genitalia or on clothing. —Is pregnant.	—Appears withdrawn or engages in fantasy or infantile behavior. —Has poor peer relationships. —Is unwilling to participate in physical activities. —Is engaging in delinquent acts or runs away. —States he/she has been sexually assaulted by parent/caretaker.	—Extremely protective or jealous of child. —Encourages child to engage in prostitution or sexual acts in the presence of caretaker. —Has been sexually abused as a child. —Is experiencing marital difficulties. —Misuses alcohol or other drugs. —Is frequently absent from the home.
Emotional Maltreatment	—Emotional maltreatment, often less tangible than other forms of child abuse and neglect, can be indicated by behaviors of the child and the caretaker.	—Appears overly compliant, passive, undemanding. —Is extremely aggressive, demanding, or rageful. —Shows overly adaptive behaviors, either inappropriately adult (e.g., parents other children) or inappropriately infantile (e.g., rocks constantly, sucks thumb, is enuretic). —Lags in physical, emotional, and intellectual development. Attempts suicide.	—Blames or belittles child. —Is cold and rejecting. —Withholds love. —Treats siblings unequally. —Seems unconcerned about child's problem.

INSTITUTIONAL CHILD ABUSE AND NEGLECT

1) Abuse and neglect as a result of social or institutional policies, practices, or conditions. The rather widespread practice of detaining children in adult jails is one example. Usually refers to specific institutions or populations, but may also be used to mean societal abuse or neglect. (See also SOCIETAL ABUSE AND NEGLECT)
2) Child abuse and neglect committed by an employee of a public or private institution or group home against a child in the institution or group home.

INTAKE

Process by which cases are introduced into an agency. Workers are usually assigned to interview persons seeking help in order to determine the nature and extent of the problem(s). However, in child abuse and neglect, intake of reports of suspected cases is usually by telephone and an interview with the reporting person is not required. Child abuse and neglect workers who do intake must be skilled in getting as much information as possible from the reporter in order to determine whether the situation is an emergency requiring instant attention.

INTERDISCIPLINARY TEAM (See COMMUNITY TEAM)

INTRADERMAL HEMORRHAGE

Bleeding within the skin; bruise. Bruises are common injuries exhibited by battered children, and are usually classified by size:

Petechiae
Very small bruise caused by broken capillaries. Petechiae may be traumatic in nature or may be caused by clotting disorders.

Purpura
Petechiae occurring in groups, or a small bruise (up to 1 cm. in diameter).

Ecchymosis
Larger bruise.

INVOLUNTARY CLIENT

Person who has been referred or court-ordered for services but who has not asked for help. Most abusive and neglectful parents are initially involuntary clients and may not accept the need for services. They may deny that there is a problem and resist assistance. Motivation for change may be minimal or nonexistent; however, skillful workers have demonstrated that motivation can be developed and treatment can be effective.

INVOLUNTARY PLACEMENT

Court-ordered assignment of custody to an agency and placement of a child, often against the parents' wishes, after a formal court proceeding, or the taking of emergency or protective custody against the parents' wishes preceding a custody hearing. (See also CUSTODY)

JEJUNUM

Middle portion of the small intestine between the duodenum and the ileum.

JURISDICTION

The power of a particular court to hear cases involving certain categories of persons or allegations. Jurisdiction may also depend upon geographical factors such as the county of a person's residence. (See also COURTS)

JURY

Group of adults selected by lawyers who judge the truth of allegations made in a legal proceeding. Trial by jury is available in all criminal cases, including cases of suspected child abuse and neglect. Very few juvenile, probate, or domestic relations court cases can be tried before a jury and are instead decided by the presiding judge.

JUVENILE COURT (See COURTS)

JUVENILE JUDGE

Presiding officer of a juvenile court. Often in a juvenile court, there are several other hearing officers of lesser rank, usually called referees or commissioners. (See also HEARING OFFICER)

LABELING
The widespread public and professional practice of affixing terms which imply serious or consistent deviance to the perpetrators and/or victims of child abuse and neglect; for example, "child abuser." Since deviance may suggest that punishment is warranted, this kind of labeling decreases the possibility of treatment. This is unfortunate, because experts agree that 80% or 85% of all child abuse and neglect cases have the potential for successful treatment. Such labeling may also make parents see themselves in a negative, despairing way, and discourage them from seeking assistance.

LABORATORY TESTS
Routine medical tests used to aid diagnosis. Those particularly pertinent to child abuse are:

Partial Thromboplastin Time (PTT) Measures clotting factors in the blood.

Prothrombin Time (PT)
Measures clotting factors in the blood.

Urinalysis
Examination of urine for sugar, protein, blood, etc.

Complete Blood Count (CBC)
Measure and analysis of red and white blood cells.

Rumpel-Leede (Tourniquet) Test
Measures fragility of capillaries and/or bruisability.

LACERATION
A jagged cut or wound.

LATCH KEY CHILDREN
Working parents' children who return after school to a home where no parent or caretaker is present. This term was coined because these children often wear a house key on a chain around their necks.

LATERAL
Toward the side.

LAY THERAPIST (See PARENT AIDE)

LEAST DETRIMENTAL ALTERNATIVE
(See
BEST INTEREST OF THE CHILD)

LEGAL RIGHTS OF PERSONS IDENTIFIED IN REPORTS
Standards for legal rights stress the need for all persons concerned with child abuse and neglect to be aware of the legal rights of individuals identified in reports and to be committed to any action necessary to enforce these rights. According to the National Center on Child Abuse and Neglect *Revision to Federal Standards on the Prevention and Treatment of Child Abuse and Neglect (Draft)*, these rights include the following:

1. Any person identified in a report as being suspected of having abused or neglected a child should be informed of his/her legal rights.
2) The person responsible for the child's welfare should receive written notice and be advised of his her legal rights when protective custody authority is exercised.
3) A child who is alleged to be abused or neglected should have independent legal representation in a child protection proceeding.
4) The parent or other person responsible for a child's welfare who is alleged to have abused or neglected a child should be entitled to legal representation in a civil or criminal proceeding.
5) The local child protective services unit should have the assistance of legal counsel in all child protective proceedings.
6) Each party should have the right to appeal protective case determinations.
7) Any person identified in a child abuse or neglect report should be protected from unauthorized disclosure of personal information contained in the report.

LESION
Any injury to any part of the body from any cause that results in damage or loss of structure or function of the body tissue involved. A lesion may be caused by poison, infection, dysfunction, or violence, and may be either accidental or intentional.

LIABILITY FOR FAILURE TO REPORT
State statutes which require certain categories of persons to report cases of suspected child abuse and/or neglect are often enforced by the imposition of a penalty, fine and/or imprisonment, for those who fail to report. Recent lawsuits have provided what may become an even more significant penalty for failure to report: when a report should have been made and a child comes to serious harm in a subsequent incident of abuse or neglect, the person who failed to report the initial incident may be held civilly liable to the child for the damages suffered in the subsequent incident. Such damages could amount to many thousands of dollars. (See also MANDATED REPORTERS)

LICENSING PARENTHOOD
Proposed method of assuring adequate parenting skills. Various proposals have been developed, including mandatory parenthood education in high school, with a certificate upon completion. Serious advocates compare the process with certification of driving capability by driver's licenses. Many consider the proposal unworkable.

LOCAL AUTHORITY
Local authority refers to two groups: 1) the social service agency (local agency) designated by the state department of social services (state department) and authorized by state law to be responsible for local child abuse and neglect prevention, identification, and treatment efforts, and 2) the community child protection coordinating council (community council). The standards on local authority, as specified in the National Center on Child Abuse and Neglect *Revision to Federal Standards on the Prevention and Treatment of Child Abuse and Neglect (Draft)*, include:

Administration and Organization
1. The local agency should establish a distinct child protective services unit with sufficient and qualified staff.
2. The local agency in cooperation with the state department should allocate sufficient funds and provide adequate administrative support to the local unit.
3. The local agency should initiate the establishment of a community council which is to be representative of those persons providing or concerned with child abuse and neglect prevention, identification, and treatment services.

Primary Prevention
4. The local unit and the community council should work together to establish formalized needs assessment and planning processes.

Secondary and Tertiary Prevention
5. The local unit and the community council should work together to develop a comprehensive and coordinated service delivery system for children-at-risk and families-at-risk to be presented in an annual plan.
6. The local unit and the community council should develop standards on the care of children which represent the minimum expectations of the community and provide the basis for the local unit's operational definitions and referral guidelines.
7. The local unit and the community council should establish a multidisciplinary child abuse and neglect case consultation team.
8. The local unit should provide or arrange for services to assist families who request help for themselves in fulfilling their parenting responsibilities.
9. The local unit should ensure that reports of child abuse and neglect can be received on a twenty-four hour, seven days per week basis.

10 The intake services worker should intervene immediately if a report is considered an emergency; otherwise, intervention should take place within seventy-two hours.
11 The intake services worker should ensure the family's right to privacy by making the assessment process time-limited.
12 The treatment services worker should develop an individualized treatment plan for each family and each family member.
13 The treatment services worker should arrange for, coordinate, and monitor services provided to a family.

Resource Enhancement

14 The agency and the community council should assist in the training of the local unit and other community service systems.
15 The agency should promote internal agency coordination.
16 The local unit should implement community education and awareness.
17 The agency should participate in or initiate its own research, review, and evaluation studies.

(See also STATE AUTHORITY)

LONG BONE
General term applied to the bones of the leg or the arm.

LONG TERM TREATMENT
Supportive and therapeutic services over a period of time, usually at least a year, to restore the parent(s) of an abused or neglected child and/or the child himself/herself to adequate levels of functioning and to prevent recurrence of child abuse or neglect.

LUMBAR
Pertaining to the part of the back and sides between the lowest ribs and the pelvis.

MALNUTRITION
Failure to receive adequate nourishment. Often exhibited in a neglected child, malnutrition may be caused by inadequate diet (either lack of food or insufficient amounts of needed vitamins, etc.) or by a disease or other abnormal condition affecting the body's ability to properly process foods taken in.

MALTREATMENT
Actions that are abusive, neglectful, or otherwise threatening to a child's welfare. Frequently used as a general term for child abuse and neglect.

MANDATED AGENCY
Agency designated by state statutes as legally responsible for receiving and investigating reports of suspected child abuse and neglect. Usually, this agency is a county welfare department or a child protective services unit within that department. Police or sheriffs departments may also be mandated agencies. (See also STATE AUTHORITY and LOCAL AUTHORITY)

MANDATED REPORTERS or MANDATORY REPORTERS
Persons designated by state statutes who are legally liable for not reporting suspected cases of child abuse and neglect to the mandated agency. The persons so designated vary according to state law, but they are primarily professionals, such as pediatricians, nurses, school personnel, and social workers, who have frequent contact with children and families.

MARASMUS
A form of protein-calorie malnutrition occurring in infants and children. It is characterized by retarded growth and progressive wasting away of fat and muscle, but it is usually accompanied by the retention of appetite and mental alertness.

MATERNAL CHARACTERISTICS SCALE
Instrument designed to study personality characteristics of rural Appalachian mothers and the level of care they were providing their children. The purpose of this scale is to

sharpen caseworkers' perception of "apathetic-futile" or "impulse-ridden" mothers' personality characteristics for evaluation, diagnosis, and formulation of a treatment plan in cases of child neglect. Some authorities believe this scale has not been adequately validated.

MATERNAL-INFANT BONDING (See BONDING)

MEDIAL
Toward the middle or mid-line.

MEDICAID, TITLE 19 (See SOCIAL SECURITY ACT)

MEDICAL MODEL
Conceptualizing problems in terms of diagnosis and treatment of illness. With respect to child abuse and neglect, the medical model assumes an identifiable and therefore treatable cause of the abuse and/or neglect and focuses on identification and treatment in a medical or other health setting. For child abuse and neglect, some advantages of the medical model are financial support by the hospital, clinic, medical community; accessibility of medical services to the abused or neglected child; involvement of the physicians; and visibility and public acceptance. Possible disadvantages are overemphasis on physical abuse; overemphasis on physical diagnosis to the detriment of total treatment; and isolation from other professional and community resources. (Kempe)

MEDICAL NEGLECT (See CHILD ABUSE AND NEGLECT)

MENKES KINKY HAIR SYNDROME
Rare, inherited disease resulting in brittle bones and, eventually, death. It is found in infants and, because of the great number of fractures the child may exhibit, can be mistaken for child abuse.

MENTAL INJURY
Injury to the intellectual or psychological capacity of a child as evidenced by observable and substantial impairment in his/her ability to function within a normal range of performance and behavior, with due regard to his/her culture. The Child Abuse Prevention and Treatment Act and some state statutes include mental injury caused by a parent or caretaker as child abuse or neglect.

MESENTERY
Membrane attaching various organs to the body wall.

METABOLISM
The sum of all physical and chemical processes which maintain the life of an organism.

METAPHYSIS
Wider part of a long bone between the end and the shaft.

MINIMALLY ACCEPTABLE ENVIRONMENT
The emotional climate and physical surroundings necessary for children to grow physically, mentally, socially, and emotionally.

MINOR (See CHILD)

MIRANDA RULE
Legal provision that a confession is inadmissible in any court proceeding if the suspect was not forewarned of his/her right to remain silent before the confession was disclosed. (See also FIFTH AMENDMENT)

MISDEMEANOR
A crime for which the punishment can be no more than imprisonment for a year and/or a fine of $1,000. A misdemeanor is distinguished from a felony, which is more serious, and an infraction, which is less serious.

MODEL CHILD PROTECTION ACT
Guide for development of state legislation concerning child abuse and neglect and intended to enable legislators to provide a

comprehensive and workable law which will aid in resolving the problem. A draft *Model Child Protection Act* has been developed and is available from the National Center on Child Abuse and Neglect.

MONDALE ACT (See CHILD ABUSE PREVENTION AND TREATMENT ACT)

MONGOLIAN SPOTS
A type of birthmark that can appear anywhere on a child's body, most frequently on the lower back. These dark spots usually fade by age five. They can be mistaken for bruises.

MORAL NEGLECT (See CHILD ABUSE AND NEGLECT)

MORIBUND
Dying or near death.

MOTHERS ANONYMOUS
Original name of Parents Anonymous. (See PARENTS ANONYMOUS)

MULTIDISCIPLINARY TEAM
A group of professionals and possibly paraprofessionals representing a variety of disciplines who interact and coordinate their efforts to diagnose and treat specific cases of child abuse and neglect. A multidisciplinary group which also addresses the general problem of child abuse and neglect in a given community is usually described as a community team, and it will probably consist of several multidisciplinary teams with different functions (see COMMUNITY TEAM). Multidisciplinary teams may include, but are not limited to, medical, child care, and law enforcement personnel, social workers, psychiatrists and/or psychologists. Their goal is to pool their respective skills in order to formulate accurate diagnoses and to provide comprehensive coordinated treatment with continuity and follow-up for both parent(s) and child or children. Many multidisciplinary teams operate according to the Denver Model (see DENVER MODEL). Multidisciplinary teams may also be referred to as cross-disciplinary teams, interdisciplinary teams, or SCAN teams (see SCAN TEAM). However, the Child Abuse Prevention and Treatment Act uses the term "multidisciplinary team."

NATIONAL ASSOCIATION OF SOCIAL WORKERS (NASW)
1425 H St., N.W.
Washington, D.C. 20005
A national organization of professional social workers who are enrolled in or have completed baccalaureate, master's, or doctoral programs in social work education. Members must subscribe to the NASW Code of Ethics, and NASW provides a policy for adjudication of grievances in order to protect members and promote ethical practices.

NATIONAL CENTER FOR CHILD ADVOCACY (NCCA)
P.O. Box 1182
Washington, D.C. 20013
The National Center for Child Advocacy is part of the Children's Bureau of the Administration for Children, Youth and Families within the Office of Human Development Services of HEW. NCCA supports research, demonstration, and training programs and provides technical assistance to state and local agencies with the goal of increasing and improving child welfare services. These services include in-home support to families, such as parent education and homemaker services; foster care, adoption, and child protective services; and institutional care of children. A major project of NCCA is the Child Welfare Resource Information Exchange. (See also CHILD WELFARE RESOURCE INFORMATION EXCHANGE)

NATIONAL CENTER FOR THE PREVENTION AND TREATMENT OF CHILD ABUSE AND NEGLECT
1205 Oneida St.
Denver, Colorado 80220
This center, which is affiliated with the Department of Pediatrics of the University of Colorado Medical School, was established in

the fall of 1972 to provide more extensive and up-to-date education, research, and clinical material to professionals working in the area of child abuse and neglect. The center's multidisciplinary staff has provided leadership in formulating the views that child abuse and neglect is symptomatic of troubled family relationships; that treatment must consider the needs of all family members; and that outreach to isolated, non-trusting families and the multidisciplinary approach are necessary. Funded by the State of Colorado, the HEW Administration for Children, Youth and Families, and private foundations, the center's work includes education, consultation and technical assistance, demonstration programs for treatment, program evaluation, and research. This center also serves as the HEW Region VIII Resource Center.

NATIONAL CENTER ON CHILD ABUSE AND NEGLECT (NCCAN)

P.O. Box 1182
Washington, D.C. 20013

Office of the federal government located within the Children's Bureau of the Administration for Children, Youth and Families (formerly the Office of Child Development), which is part of the Office of Human Development Services of HEW. Established in 1974 by the Child Abuse Prevention and Treatment Act, the functions of NCCAN are to:

1) Compile, analyze, and publish an annual summary of recent and current research on child abuse and neglect.
2) Develop and maintain an information clearinghouse on all programs showing promise of success for the prevention, identification, and treatment of child abuse and neglect.
3) Compile and publish training materials for personnel who are engaged or intend to engage in the prevention, identification, and treatment of child abuse and neglect.
4) Provide technical assistance to public and nonprofit private agencies and organizations to assist them in planning, improving, developing, and carrying out programs and activities relating to the prevention, identification, and treatment of child abuse and neglect.
5) Conduct research into the causes of child abuse and neglect, and into the prevention, identification, and treatment thereof.
6) Make a complete and full study and investigation of the national incidence of child abuse and neglect, including a determination of the extent to which incidents of child abuse and neglect are increasing in number or severity.
7) Award grants to states whose child abuse and neglect legislation complies with federal legislation.

NCCAN is authorized to establish grants and contracts with public and private agencies and organizations to carry out the above activities. Grants and contracts may also be used to establish demonstration programs and projects which, through training, consultation, resource provision, or direct treatment, are designed to prevent, identify, and treat child abuse and neglect. (See also CHILD ABUSE PREVENTION AND TREATMENT ACT and REGIONAL RESOURCE CENTER)

NATIONAL CLEARINGHOUSE ON CHILD NEGLECT AND ABUSE (NCCNA) (See NATIONAL STUDY ON CHILD NEGLECT AND ABUSE REPORTING)

NATIONAL COMMITTEE FOR THE PREVENTION OF CHILD ABUSE

111 E. Wacker Drive
Suite 510
Chicago, Illinois 60601

The National Committee originated in Chicago in 1972 in response to increasing national incidence of deaths due to child abuse. It was formed to help prevent child abuse, which was defined as including non-accidental injury, emotional abuse, neglect, sexual abuse, and exploitation of children, at a time when most programs focused on identification and treatment. The commit-

tee's goals are to:
1) Stimulate greater public awareness of the problem.
2) Encourage public involvement in prevention and treatment.
3) Provide a national focal point for advocacy to prevent child abuse.
4) Facilitate communication about programs, policy, and research related to child abuse prevention.
5) Foster greater cooperation between existing and developing resources for child abuse prevention.

Activities of the committee include a national media campaign, publications, conference, research, and the establishment of state chapters of the committee.

NATIONAL REGISTER
Often confused with the National Study on Child Neglect and Abuse Reporting (National Clearinghouse), which compiles statistics on incidence of child abuse and neglect. A national register, which does not exist at this time, would operate in much the same way and with the same purposes as a state-level central register, but would collect reports of abuse and neglect nationwide. Collecting reports on a national scale would be highly problematic because of variance in state reporting laws and definitions of abuse and neglect. (See also CENTRAL REGISTER and NATIONAL STUDY ON CHILD NEGLECT AND ABUSE REPORTING)

NATIONAL STUDY ON CHILD NEGLECT AND ABUSE REPORTING
Formerly the National Clearinghouse on Child Neglect and Abuse, the National Study is funded by the National Center on Child Abuse and Neglect, Children's Bureau, HEW and is being conducted by the Children's Division of the American Humane Association. The study has been established to systematically collect data from official state sources on the nature, incidence, and characteristics of child abuse and neglect. Participating states receive reports generated from their own data on a quarterly basis so that they can monitor their own reporting mechanisms. At this time, about 40 states are submitting detailed incidence data to the study. It is hoped that the National Study will be able to produce accurate data on the national incidence of child abuse and neglect.

NEEDS ASSESSMENT
A formal or informal evaluation of what services are needed by abused and neglected children and their families within a specified geographical area or within another given population.

NEGLECT (See CHILD ABUSE AND NEGLECT)

NEGLECTED CHILD (See INDICATORS OF CHILD ABUSE AND NEGLECT)

NEGLIGENCE
Failure to act. May apply to a parent, as in child neglect, or to a person who by state statute is mandated to report child abuse and neglect but who fails to do so. Negligence lawsuits arising from failure to report are increasing, and any failure to obey the statutes proves negligence. Lawsuits claiming damages for negligence are civil proceedings.

NETWORKING
Formal or informal linkages of individuals, families, or other groups with similar social, education, medical, or other service needs with the public or private agencies, organizations, and/or individuals who can provide such services in their locale. Formal agreements are usually written and spell out under what circumstances a particular agency, group, or individual will provide certain services. Informal agreements are apt to be verbal and relate to a particular family or case.

NURTURANCE
Affectionate care and attention provided by a parent, parent substitute, or caretaker to promote the well-being of a child and encour-

age healthy emotional and physical development. Nurturance may also be needed by adults with inadequate parenting skills, or who were themselves abused or neglected as children, as a model for developing more positive relationships with their own children and as a way of strengthening their own self-esteem.

OCCIPITAL
Referring to the back of the head.

OMISSION, ACTS OF
Failure of a parent or caretaker to provide for a child's physical and/or emotional well-being. (See also CHILD ABUSE AND NEGLECT)

OSSIFICATION
Formation of bone.

OSTEOGENESIS IMPERFECTA
An inherited condition in which the bones are abnormally brittle and subject to fractures, and which may be mistakenly diagnosed as the result of child abuse.

OUTREACH
The process in which professionals, paraprofessionals, and/or volunteers actively seek to identify cases of family strees and potential or actual child abuse and neglect by making services known, accessible, and unthreatening. Effective outreach providing early intervention is important for the prevention of child abuse and neglect.

PA BUDDY
Term used by Parents Anonymous for a person who functions like a parent aide in relation to a Parents Anonymous member. (See also PARENTS ANONYMOUS and PARENT AIDE)

PARAPROFESSIONAL
Volunteer or agency employee trained to a limited extent in a particular profession. Since paraprofessionals are usually close in age, race, nationality, religion, or lifestyle to the clientele, they often have a greater likelihood of developing a trusting relationship with a client than do some professionals. The role of the paraprofessional in protective service work is usually to provide outreach or nurturance and advocacy for the family, often as a case aide or parent aide. (See also PARENT AIDE)

PARENS PATRIAE
"The power of the sovereign." Refers to the state's power to act for or on behalf of persons who cannot act in their own behalf; such as, minors, incompetents, or some developmentally disabled.

PARENT
Person exercising the function of father and/or mother, including adoptive, foster, custodial, and surrogate parents as well as biological parents.

PARENT AIDE
A paraprofessional, either paid or voluntary, who functions primarily as an advocate and surrogate parent for a family in which child abuse or neglect is suspected or has been confirmed. The Parent Aide particularly serves the mother by providing positive reinforcement, emotional support, and nurturance, and by providing or arranging transportation, babysitting, etc., as necessary. Rather than serving as a homemaker, nutrition aide, or nurse, the parent aide's function is more like a friend to the family. Parent aides may also be referred to as case aides, lay therapists, or visiting friends.

PARENT EFFECTIVENESS TRAINING (PET)
An educational program developed by Dr. Thomas Gordon and presented in his book, *Parent Effectiveness Training* (New York, Peter H. Wyden, Inc., 1970). The program, taught by trained and certified PET instructors, focuses on improving communication between parents and children by teaching listening skills and verbal expression techniques to parents. The PET course has proven useful for parents who are motivated to change, who are able to give it a consider-

able amount of time, and who can afford the relatively high tuition. For these and other reasons, PET has not proven particularly useful in child abuse and neglect treatment, especially when used as the only mode of treatment.

PARENTAL STRESS SERVICES

Services aimed at relieving situational and/or psychological parental stress in order to relieve family dysfunction and to prevent parents from venting rage or frustration on their children. Service usually begins via a telephone helpline and may include home visits. Workers are usually trained volunteers or paraprofessionals who focus on providing warmth, nurturance, friendship, and resource referrals to the distressed parent. Some parental stress services promote development and use of Parents Anonymous chapters for their clients. Parental Stress Services may refer to specific programs such as in Chicago, Illinois, or Oakland, California, although there is no organizational linkage between them, or this may be a functional description of services provided within a larger agency program.

PARENTING SKILLS

A parent's competencies in providing physical care, protection, supervision, and psychological nurturance appropriate to a child's age and stage of development. Some parents, particularly those whose own parents demonstrated these skills, have these competencies without formal training, but adequacy of these skills may be improved through instruction.

PARENTS ANONYMOUS
22330 Hawthorne Blvd., #208
Torrance, California 90505

Self-help group for parents who want to stop physical, psychological, sexual, or verbal abuse of their children. Because members do not need to reveal their full names, they feel free to share concerns and provide mutual support. Members are accountable to the group for their behavior toward their children, and the group functions like a family in supporting members' efforts to change. With chapters in every state, over 800 in all, Parents Anonymous has been formally evaluated as an effective method for treating child abuse. Unlike most other self-help groups with anonymous members, Parents Anonymous requires that each chapter have an unpaid professional sponsor who attends all meetings to facilitate discussion, provide a role model, and suggest appropriate community resources for members' problems. The Child Abuse Prevention and Treatment Act provides for funding of self-help groups, and Parents Anonymous is one of the few self-help organizations which has received funding from the federal government.

PARENTS' RIGHTS

Besides the rights protected by the Constitution for all adults, society accords parents the right to custody and supervision of their own children, including, among others, parents' rights to make decisions about their children's health care. This plus parents' rights to privacy may complicate investigations of suspected child abuse and neglect and treatment of confirmed cases. Parents' rights may be cited in court in order to prevent the state from taking custody of a child who is in danger in his/her own home. (See also CHILDREN'S RIGHTS)

PARENTS UNITED

Organization name sometimes used for self-help groups of parents in families in which sexual abuse has occurred. Begun in 1972, Parents United is one component of a model Child Sexual Abuse Treatment Program in Santa Clara County, California. (See also DAUGHTERS UNITED)

PASSIVE ABUSER

Parent or caretaker who does not intervene to prevent abuse by another person in the home.

PATHOGNOMONIC

A sign or symptom specifically distinctive or characteristic of a disease or condition from which a diagnosis may be made.

PERINATAL
Around the time of birth, both immediately before and afterward.

PERIOSTEAL ELEVATION
The ripping or tearing of the surface layer of a bone (periosteum) and the resultant hemorrhage, occuring when a bone is broken.

PERITONITIS
Inflammation of the membrane lining the abdomen (peritoneum); caused by infection.

PERJURY
Intentionally inaccurate testimony. Perjury is usually punishable as a felony, but only if the inaccuracy of the testimony and the witness's knowledge of the inaccuracy can be proven.

PETECHIAE (See INTRADERMAL HEMORRHAGE)

PETITION
Document filed in juvenile or family court at the beginning of a neglect, abuse, and/or delinquency case. The petition states the allegations which, if true, form the basis for court intervention.

PETITIONER
Person who files a petition. In juvenile and family court practice, a petitioner may be a probation officer, social worker, or prosecutor, as variously defined by state laws.

PHYSICAL ABUSE (See CHILD ABUSE AND NEGLECT)

PHYSICAL NEGLECT (See CHILD ABUSE AND NEGLECT)

PLEA BARGAINING
Settlement of a criminal prosecution, usually by the reduction of the charge and/or the penalty, in return for a plea of guilty. Plea bargains are sometimes justified by congested court calendars. They are attacked as devices which weaken the intended effect of penal statutes and which reduce the dignity of the criminal justice system. Far more than half of all criminal prosecutions in this country are resolved by plea bargaining.

POLICE HOLD (See CUSTODY)

POLYPHAGIA
Excessive or voracious eating.

PREDICTION OF CHILD ABUSE AND NEGLECT
There are no evaluation instruments or criteria to predict absolutely that child abuse or neglect will occur in specific families. Recently, experts have developed instruments and methods of evaluating the bonding process at childbirth in order to identify families where because of incomplete or inadequate bonding, it can be expected that without further appropriate intervention, child abuse or neglect may occur. Besides bonding, many other indicators can be used to identify families-at-risk for child abuse and neglect, but these factors are rarely sufficiently conclusive to enable absolute prediction. (See also BONDING and FAMILIES-AT-RISK)

PREPONDERANCE OF EVIDENCE (See EVIDENTIARY STANDARDS)

PRESENTMENT
The notice taken or report made by a grand jury of an offense on the basis of the jury's knowledge and without a bill of indictment. (See also INDICTMENT)

PRE-TRIAL DIVERSION
Decision of the district attorney not to issue charges in a criminal case where those charges would be provable. The decision is usually made on the condition that the defendant agrees to participate in rehabilitative services. In child abuse cases, this usually involves cooperation with child protective services and/or voluntary treatment, such as Parents Anonymous.

PREVENTION OF CHILD ABUSE AND NEGLECT

Elimination of the individual and societal causes of child abuse and neglect.

Primary Prevention
Providing societal and community policies and programs which strengthen all family functioning so that child abuse and neglect is less likely to occur.

Secondary Prevention
Intervention in the early signs of child abuse and neglect for treatment of the presenting problem and to prevent further problems from developing.

Tertiary Prevention
Treatment after child abuse and neglect has been confirmed.

Primary, and to varying degrees secondary and tertiary, prevention requires:

1) Breaking the tendency in the generational cycle wherein the abused or neglected child is likely to become the abusive or neglectful parent.
2) Helping a parent cope with a child who has special problems or special meaning to a parent.
3) Helping families cope with long term and immediate situational or interpersonal stress.
4) Linking families to personal and community sources of help to break their social isolation.
5) Eliminating or alleviating violence in our society, particularly sanctioned violence such as corporal punishment in the schools.

A major problem in preventing child abuse and neglect is the stigma attached to the problem and to receiving services from a county protective service agency. Therefore, prevention programs must include community education and outreach. Another problem is that stress is pervasive in our society, and ways must be found both to reduce it and deal with it if child abuse and neglect is to be prevented. (See also EARLY INTERVENTION)

PRIMA FACIE

A latin term approximately meaning "at first sight," "on the first appearance," or "on the face of it." In law, this term is used in the context of a "prima facie case." That is, the presentation of evidence at a trial which has been sufficiently strong to prove the allegations unless contradicted and overcome by other evidence. In a child maltreatment case, the allegations of maltreatment will be considered as proven unless the parent presents rebutting evidence.

PRIVILEGED COMMUNICATIONS

Confidential communications which are protected by statutes and need not or cannot be disclosed in court over the objections of the holder of the privilege. Lawyers are almost always able to refuse to disclose what a client has told them in confidence. Priests are similarly covered. Doctors and psychotherapists have generally lesser privileges, and their testimony can be compelled in many cases involving child abuse or neglect. Some social workers are covered by such statutes, but the law and practice vary widely from state to state. (See also CONFIDENTIALITY)

PROBABLE CAUSE

A legal standard used in a number of contexts which indicates a reasonable ground for suspicion or belief in the existence of certain facts. Facts accepted as true after a reasonable inquiry which would induce a prudent and cautious person to believe them. Also-Please note that the definitions on page 28 of EVIDENTIARY STANDARDS are incorrect. A suggested alternative follows:

PROBATE COURT (See COURTS)

PROBATION

Allowing a convicted criminal defendant or a juvenile found to be delinquent to remain at liberty, under a suspended sentence of imprisonment, generally under the supervision of a probation officer and under certain conditions. Violation of a condition is grounds for revocation of the probation. In a case of child abuse or neglect, a parent or caretaker who is convicted of the offense may be required, as part of his/her probation, to make certain promises to undergo treatment and/or to improve the home situation. These promises are made as a condition of the probation in which the child is returned home and are enforced with the threat of revocation of parental rights.

PROGRAM COORDINATION
Interagency of intra-agency communication for policy, program, and resource development for an effective service delivery system in a given locality. Program coordination for child abuse and neglect is usually implemented through a community council or community task force or planning committee under the direction of a program coordinator. The functions of these groups are:
1) Comprehensive planning, including identifying gaps and duplication in service and funding policies.
2) Developing interagency referral policies.
3) Educating members to new and/or effective approaches to child abuse and neglect.
4) Problem sharing.
5) Facilitating resolution of interagency conflicts.
6) Providing a forum where differing professional and agency expertise can be pooled.
7) Generating and lobbying for needed legislation.
(See also COMMUNITY TEAM)

PROTECTIVE CUSTODY (See CUSTODY)

PROTOCOL
A set of rules or guidelines prescribing procedures and responsibilities. Originally used primarily in medical settings, establishment of protocols is an increasingly important goal of the child abuse and neglect community team.

PROXIMAL
Near; closer to any point of reference; opposed to distal.

PSYCHOLOGICAL ABUSE (See CHILD ABUSE AND NEGLECT)

PSYCHOLOGICAL NEGLECT (See CHILD ABUSE AND NEGLECT)

PSYCHOLOGICAL PARENT
Adult who, on a continuing day-to-day basis, fulfills a child's emotional needs for nurturance through interaction, companionship, and mutuality. May be the natural parent or another person who fulfills these functions.

PSYCHOLOGICAL TESTS
Instruments of various types used to measure emotional, intellectual, and personality characteristics. Psychological tests should always be administered and interpreted by qualified personnel. Such tests have been used to determine potential for abuse or neglect, effects of abuse or neglect, or psychological makeup of parent or children.

PSYCHOTIC PARENT
A parent who suffers a major mental disorder where the individual's ability to think, respond emotionally, remember, communicate, interpret reality, or behave appropriately is sufficiently impaired so as to interfere grossly with his/her capacity to meet the ordinary demands of life. The term "psychotic" is neither very precise nor definite. However, the parent who is periodically psychotic or psychotic for extended periods and who abuses his/her children has a poor prognosis; permanent removal of the children is often recommended in this situation. It is estimated that well under 10% of all abusive or neglectful parents are psychotic.

PUBLIC AWARENESS (See COMMUNITY AWARENESS)

PUBLIC DEFENDER
Person paid with public funds to plead the cause of an indigent defendant.

PUBLIC LAW 93-247 (See CHILD ABUSE PREVENTION AND TREATMENT ACT)

PUNISHMENT
Infliction of pain, loss, or suffering on a child because the child has disobeyed or otherwise antagonized a parent or caretaker. Abusive parents may inflict punishment without cause, or may inflict punishment, particularly corporal punishment, in the belief that it is the only way to discipline children. Many parents confuse the difference between discipline and punishment. These differences are delineated under DISCIPLINE. (See also CORPORAL PUNISHMENT)

PURCHASE OF SERVICE
Provision for diagnosis and/or treatment of child abuse and neglect by an agency other than the mandated agency using mandated agency funds. The mandated agency subcontracts with the provider agency for specific services with specific clients, but the mandated agency retains statutory responsibility for the case. (See also CASE MANAGEMENT)

PURPURA (See INTRADERMAL HEMORRHAGE)

RADIOLUCENT
Permitting the passage of X-rays without leaving a shadow on the film. Soft tissues are radiolucent; bones are not.

RAREFACTION
Loss of density. On an X-ray photograph, an area of bone which appears lighter than normal is in a state of rarefaction, indicating a loss of calcium.

RECEIVING HOME
A family or group home for temporary placement of a child pending more permanent plans such as return to his/her own home, foster care, or adoption.

RECIDIVISM
Recurrence of child abuse and neglect. This happens relatively frequently because child protective service agencies heretofore have been mandated and staffed only to investigate and provide crisis intervention and not to provide treatment. Most cases where child abuse or neglect results in a child's death have been previously known to a child protection agency.

REFEREE (See HEARING OFFICER)

REGIONAL RESOURCE CENTER
With respect to child abuse and neglect, a regional resource center was funded as a demonstration project in each of the ten HEW regions under the 1974 Child Abuse Prevention and Treatment Act. These resource centers vary in program emphasis, but they all function to some degree as extensions of the National Center on Child Abuse and Neglect in Washington to help NCCAN fulfill the aims of the Child Abuse Prevention and Treatment Act (see NATIONAL CENTER ON CHILD ABUSE AND NEGLECT and CHILD ABUSE PREVENTION AND TREATMENT ACT). Besides regional centers, there are also state resource centers in Arizona, Maryland, New York, and North Carolina; and two national resource centers, operated by the Education Commission of the States and the National Urban League. The regional resource centers are:

Region I (Connecticut, Maine, Massachusetts, New Hampshire, Rhode Island, Vermont)
Judge Baker Guidance Center
295 Longwood Ave.
Boston, Massachusetts 02115
Region II (New Jersey, Puerto Rico, Virgin Islands)
College of Human Ecology Cornell University
MVR Hall
Ithaca, New York 14853
Region III (Pennsylvania, Virginia, Delaware, West Virginia, District of Columbia)
Institute for Urban Affairs and Research
Howard University

2900 Van Ness St., N.W.
Washington, D.C. 20008
Region IV (Alabama, Florida, Georgia, Kentucky, Mississippi, South Carolina, Tennessee)
Regional Institute of Social Welfare Research
P.O. Box 152
Heritage Building
468 N. Milledge Ave.
Athens, Georgia 30601
Region V (Illinois, Indiana, Michigan, Minnesota, Ohio, Wisconsin)
Midwest Parent-Child Welfare Resource Center
Center for Advanced Studies in Human Services
School of Social Welfare
University of Wisconsin-Milwaukee
Milwaukee, Wisconsin 53201
Region VI (Arkansas, Louisiana, New Mexico, Oklahoma, Texas)
Center for Social Work Research
School of Social Work
University of Texas at Austin
Austin, Texas 78712
Region VII (Iowa, Kansas, Missouri, Nebraska)
Institute of Child Behavior and Development
University of Iowa
Oakdale, Iowa 53219
Region VIII (Colorado, Montana, North Dakota, South Dakota, Utah, Wyoming)
National Center for the Prevention and Treatment of Child Abuse and Neglect
University of Colorado Medical Center
1205 Oneida St.
Denver, Colorado 80220
Region IX (California, Hawaii, Nevada, Guam, Trust Territories of the Pacific, American Samoa)
Department of Special Education
California State University
5151 State University Dr.
Los Angeles, California 90033
Region X (Alaska, Idaho, Oregon, Washington)
Northwest Federation for Human Services
157 Yesler Way, #208
Seattle, Washington 98104

REGISTRY (See CENTRAL REGISTER and NATIONAL REGISTER)

REHEARING
After a juvenile court referee or commissioner has heard a case and made an order, some states permit a dissatisfied party to request another hearing before the supervising judge of juvenile court. This second hearing is called a rehearing. If the original hearing was not recorded by a court reporter, the rehearing may have to be granted. If a transcript exists, the judge may read it and either grant or deny the rehearing.

REPARENTING
Usually describes a nurturing process whereby parents who have not received adequate nurturance during their own childhoods are provided with emotional warmth and security through a surrogate parent such as a parent aide. Abusive and neglectful parents are thus given an opportunity to identify with more positive role models.

REPORTING LAWS
State laws which require specified categories of persons, such as professionals involved with children, and allow other persons, to notify public authorities of cases of suspected child abuse and, sometimes, neglect. All 50 states now have reporting statutes, but they differ widely with respect to types of instances which must be reported, persons who must report, time limits for reporting, manner of reporting (written, oral, or both), agencies to which reports must be made, and the degree of immunity conferred upon reporters.

RES IPSA LOQUITOR
Latin expression meaning "the thing speaks for itself." It is a doctrine of law which, when applied to criminal law, means that evidence can be admitted which is acceptable despite the fact that no one actually saw what occurred, only the results. An example in

criminal law would be admitting into evidence in a child abuse case the medical reports of the injured child victim which reflect multiple broken bones and the doctor's opinion that said injuries could not have been caused by an accident. The court using the *res ipsa loquitor* doctrine can convict the person having had exclusive custody of the child without any direct testimony as to how, when, where, or why the injuries were inflicted.

RETINA
Inside lining of the eye. Injury to the head can cause bleeding or-detachment of the retina, possible causing blindness.

RICKETS
Condition caused by a deficiency of vitamin D, which disturbs the normal development of bones.

ROLE REVERSAL
The process whereby a parent or caretaker seeks nurturance and/or protection from a child rather than providing this for the child, who frequently complies with this reversal. Usually this process develops as a result of unfulfilled needs of the parent or caretaker.

SACRAL AREA
Lower part of the back.

SCAN TEAM
Suspected Child Abuse and Neglect team which has as its objective the assessment of a child and his/her family to determine if abuse and/or neglect has occurred and what treatment is indicated. The team usually includes a pediatrician, a social worker, and a psychiatrist or psychologist, but other professionals are often involved as well. A SCAN team or unit is generally located in a hospital or outpatient facility. (See also MULTIDISCIPLINARY TEAM and DENVER MODEL)

SCAPEGOATING
Casting blame for a problem on one who is innocent or only partially responsible; for example, a parent or caretaker abusing or neglecting a child as punishment for family problems unrelated to the child.

SCURVY
Condition caused by a deficiency of vitamin C (ascorbic acid) and characterized by weakness, anemia, spongy gums, and other symptoms.

SEALING
In juvenile court or criminal court practice, the closing of records to inspection by all but the defendant or minor involved. Sealing is provided by statute in some states and may be done after proof is made that the defendant or minor has behaved lawfully for a specified period of years. Note that juvenile court records are never public, as are the records of most other courts; access to juvenile court records is theoretically very restricted, even before sealing. (See also EXPUNGEMENT)

SEIZURES
Uncontrollable muscular contractions, usually alternating with muscular relaxation and generally accompanied by unconsciousness. Seizures, which vary in intensity and length of occurrence, are the result of some brain irritation which has been caused by disease, inherited condition, fever, tumor, vitamin deficiency, or injury to the head.

SELF-HELP GROUP
Groups of persons with similar, often stigmatized, problems who share concerns and experiences in an effort to provide mutual help to one another. Usually these groups are self-directed. (See also PARENTS ANONYMOUS)

SELF-INCRIMINATION
The giving of a statement, in court or during an investigation, which subjects the person giving the statement to criminal liability. (See also DUE PROCESS, FIFTH AMENDMENT, IMMUNITY, and MIRANDA RULE)

SENTENCING
The last stage of criminal prosecution in which a convicted defendant is ordered imprisoned, fined, or granted probation. This is equivalent in a criminal case, to the disposition in a juvenile court case.

SEQUELAE
After-effects; usually medical events following an injury or disease. In child abuse and neglect, sequelae is used to refer to psychological consequences of abusive acts and also the perpetuation of maltreatment behavior across generations, as well as specific aftereffects such as brain damage, speech impairment, and impaired physical and/or psychological growth.

SERVICES
(See EARLY INTERVENTION, EMERGENCY SERVICES, PREVENTION OF CHILD ABUSE AND NEGLECT, SUPPORTIVE SERVICES, TREATMENT OF CHILD ABUSE AND NEGLECT)

SEXUAL ABUSE
In order to encompass all forms of child sexual abuse and exploitation within its mandate, the National Center on Child Abuse and Neglect has adopted the following tentative definition of child sexual abuse: contacts or interactions between a child and an adult when the child is being used for the sexual stimulation of the perpetrator or another person. Sexual abuse may also be committed by a person under the age of 18 when that person is either significantly older than the victim or when the perpetrator is in a position of power or control over another child. (See also CHILD ABUSE AND NEGLECT)

SEXUAL ASSAULT
Unlawful actions of a sexual nature committed against a person forcibly and against his/her own will. Various degrees of sexual assault are established by state law and are distinguished by the sex of the perpetrator and/or victim, the amount of force used, the amount and type of sexual contact, etc. Sexual abuse is one form of sexual assault wherein the perpetrator is known by the victim and is usually a member of the family. (See also CHILD ABUSE AND NEGLECT)

SEXUAL EXPLOITATION
A term usually used in reference to sexual abuse of children for commercial purposes; such as child prostitution, sexual exhibition, or the production of pornographic materials. (See also CHILD PORNOGRAPHY, CHILD PROSTITUTION)

SEXUAL MISUSE
Alternative term for sexual abuse, but particularly reflects the point of view that sexual encounters with children, if properly handled, need not be as harmful as is usually assumed. Its implication is that children are not necessarily harmed by so-called sexually abusive acts themselves, but rather the abuse results from damage generated by negative social and cultural reactions to such acts. (See also CHILD MISUSE AND NEGLECT, INCEST, SEXUAL ABUSE)

SEXUALLY TRANSMISSIBLE DISEASE (STD) (See VENEREAL DISEASE)

SIMPLE FRACTURE (See FRACTURE)

SITUATIONAL CHILD ABUSE AND NEGLECT
Refers to cases of child abuse and particularly child neglect where the major causative factors cannot be readily eliminated because they relate to problems over which the parents have little control. (See also APATHY-FUTILITY SYNDROME)

SKELETAL SURVEY
A series of X-rays that studies all bones of the body. Such a survey should be done in all cases of suspected abuse to locate any old, as well as new, fractures which may exist.

SOCIAL ASSESSMENT (See ASSESSMENT)

SOCIAL HISTORY
1) Information compiled by a social worker about factors affecting a family's past and present level of functioning for use in diagnosing child abuse and neglect and developing a treatment plan.
2) Document prepared by a probation officer or social worker for the juvenile or family court hearing officer's consideration at the time of disposition of a case. This report addresses the minor's history and environment. Social histories often contain material which would clearly be inadmissible in most judicial proceedings, either because of hearsay or lack of verification or reliability. The informal use of such reports has often been attacked as in violation of due process rights of minors and parents.

SOCIAL REPORT (See SOCIAL HISTORY)

SOCIAL ISOLATION
The limited interaction and contact of many abusive and/or neglectful parents with relatives, neighbors, friends, or community resources. Social isolation can perpetuate a basic lack of trust which hinders both identification and treatment of child abuse and neglect.

SOCIAL SECURITY ACT
Established in 1935 as a national social insurance program, this federal legislation includes several sections particularly applicable to child and family welfare:

Title IV-Parts A, B, C, D (Aid to Families with Dependent Children, Child Welfare Services, Work Incentive Program, Child Support and Establishment of Paternity)
Part A, now included under Title XX as services for children, was designed to encourage families to care for dependent children in their own or relatives' homes by providing services to families below a specified income level. As a condition of receiving federal funding for this program, states must provide family planning services. Part B authorizes support to states for child welfare services developed in coordination with the AFDC program to supplement or substitute for parental care and supervision. These services include day care, foster care, and other preventive or protective programs promoting child and family welfare. Part C offers job training and placement for AFDC parents in an effort to assist them in becoming self-supporting. Part D enforces the support obligations owed by absent parents to their children by locating absent parents, establishing paternity, and obtaining child support.

Title V-Maternal and Child Health and Applied Children's Services
Provides a broad range of health care services for mothers and children from low-income families in order to reduce maternal and infant mortality and to prevent illness.

Title XIX-Grants to States for Medical Assistance Programs (Medicaid or Title 19)
Designed to help families with dependent children and other low-income persons by providing financial assistance for necessary medical services. This act is additionally designed to provide rehabilitation and other psychotherapy services to help families and individuals retain or regain independence and self-sufficiency.

Title XX-Grants to States for Services
Provides grants to states for developing programs and services designed to achieve the following goals for families and/or children: economic self-support; self-sufficiency; prevention of abuse and neglect; preserving; rehabilitating, reuniting families; referring for institutional care when other services are not appropriate.

Mandated child protective service agency programs are primarily funded through Title IV-B and Title XX of the Social Security Act.

SOCIETAL CHILD ABUSE AND NEGLECT
Failure of society to provide social policies and/or funding to support the well-being of all families and children or to provide sufficient resources to prevent and treat child

abuse and neglect, particularly for minority populations such as migrant workers and Native Americans.

SPECIAL CHILD
A child who is abused or neglected or at risk of abuse or neglect because he/she has a special problem with which the parent(s) have difficulty coping or because the child has some psychologically negative meaning for the parent. Also referred to as "target child." If this child is abused, the cause may be referred to as "victim" precipitated abuse."

SPIRAL FRACTURE (See FRACTURE)

SPOUSE ABUSE
Non-accidental physical or psychological injury inflicted on either husband or wife by his/her marital partner. Some experts conjecture that husbands as well as wives are frequently abused, particularly psychologically, but the subject of husband abuse has not gained public or professional recognition to the extent that battered wives has. Domestic violence is the term used when referring to abuse between adult mates who may not be married. (See also BATTERED WOMEN)

STAFF BURNOUT
Apathy and frustration felt by protective service workers who are overworked, undertrained, and lacking agency or supervisory support. This is a common problem, and workers who do not leave protective services (see STAFF FLIGHT) or who do not have supervisory support often lose sensitivity to client needs. (Also referred to as Worker Burnout)

STAFF FLIGHT
Continous change of child protective services staff due to staff burnout (see STAFF BURNOUT). This creates the need to provide frequent training for new workers. Informed estimates place the overall national turnover rate of protective service workers at 85% annually.

STAFF SATISFACTION
Structuring a supportive and encouraging environment for protective service workers with regular periods when no new cases are assigned, thereby decreasing staff burnout and staff flight. Supervisors and administrators need to develop programs including the following elements: manageable caseloads, in-service training, participation in and responsibility for agency decision-making.

STANDARD OF PROOF (See EVIDENTIARY STANDARDS)

STANDARDS
Guides developed to ensure comprehensiveness and adequacy of programs or services. Issued by relevant agencies, such as the National Center on Child Abuse and Neglect for state and local level programs and the Child Welfare League of America for member agencies, standards have various levels of authority.

STATE AUTHORITY
State authority refers to the state department of social services (state department) and a state child protection coordinating committee (state committee). As designated in state law, these structures are to accept responsibility for child abuse and neglect prevention, identification, and treatment efforts. The standards on state authority, as specified in the National Center on Child Abuse and Neglect *Revision to Federal Standards on the Prevention and Treatment of Child Abuse and Neglect (Draft),* include:
Administration and Organization
1. The state department should establish child abuse and neglect policies that are consistent with the state law and conducive to state-wide delivery of uniform and coordinated services.
2. The state department should establish a distinct child protection division (state division) to facilitate the implementation of departmental policies.
3. The state department should designate child protective services units

(local units) within each regional and/or local social services agency.

4. The state committee, as required by state law, should be representative of those persons and agencies concerned with child abuse and neglect prevention, identification, and treatment.

Primary Prevention

5. The state division and the state committee should work together towards primary prevention of child abuse and neglect through formalized needs assessment and planning processes.

Secondary and Tertiary Prevention

6. The state division and the state committee should jointly develop a comprehensive and coordinated plan for delivery of services to high-risk children and families.
7. The state division should ensure that those persons who have reason to suspect child abuse or neglect can make a report at any time, twenty-four hours a day, seven days a week.
8. The state division should transmit reports to appropriate authority for assessment of the degree of risk to the child.
9. The state division should operate a central registry that facilitates state and local planning.
10. The state division's operation of the central registry should ensure that children and families' rights to prompt and effective services are protected.

Resource Enhancement

11. The state division should develop and provide public and professional education.
12. The state division should ensure that training is provided to all divisional, regional, and local staff.
13. The state division should conduct and/or sponsor research, demonstration, and evaluation projects.

(See also LOCAL AUTHORITY)

STATUS OFFENSE
An act which is considered criminal only because it is committed by a person of a particular status, such as a minor. If an adult did the same thing, it would not be an offense. For example, a minor staying out after curfew.

STIPULATION
A statement, either oral or written, between lawyers on both sides of a particular court case which establishes certain facts about the case that are agreed upon by both sides. The facts delineated usually involve such issues as the addresses of the persons involved in the case, their relationships to one another, etc.

STRESS FACTORS
Environmental and/or psychological pressures over a prolonged period which are associated with child abuse and neglect or which, without being prolonged, may be the precipitant event. While a certain amount of stress can be useful in motivating people to change, it is generally agreed that there is an overload of stress in our present society, perhaps because people feel decreasingly in control of the forces affecting their lives. Prevention of child abuse and neglect requires both reducing stress in society and helping people cope with it. Environmental stress which may influence child abuse and neglect includes, but is not limited to, unemployment, poverty, poor and overcrowded housing, competition for success, and "keeping up with the Joneses." Psychological stress besides that caused by environmental factors which may influence child abuse and neglect could include such problems as marital discord, in-law problems, unwanted pregnancy, role confusion resulting from the Women's Movement, and unresolved psychodynamic conflicts from childhood.

SUBDURAL HEMATOMA
A common symptom of abused children, consisting of a collection of blood beneath the outermost membrane covering the brain and spinal cord. The hematoma may be caused by a blow to the head or from shaking a baby or small child. (See also WHIP-

LASH-SHAKEN INFANT SYNDROME)

SUBPOENA
A document issued by a court clerk, usually delivered by a process server or police officer to the person subpoenaed, requiring that person to appear at a certain court at a certain day and time to give testimony in a specified case. Failure to obey a subpoena is punishable as contempt of court.

SUBPOENA DUCES TECUM
A subpoena requiring the person subpoenaed to bring specified records to court.

SUDDEN INFANT DEATH SYNDROME (SIDS)
A condition which can be confused with child abuse, SIDS affects infants from two weeks to two years old, but usually occurs in a child less than six months of age. In SIDS, a child who has been healthy except for a minor respiratory infection is found dead, often with bloody frothy material in his/her mouth. The cause of SIDS is not fully understood. The confusion with child abuse results from the bloody sputum and occasional facial bruises that accompany the syndrome. However, SIDS parents rarely display the guarded or defensive behavior that many abusive parents do.

SUMMONS
A document issued by a court clerk, usually delivered by a process server or police officer to the person summoned, notifying that person of the filing of a lawsuit against him/her and notifying that person of the deadline for answering the suit. A summons does not require the attendance at court of any person.

SUPERVISION
1) Provision of age-appropriate protection and guidance for a child by a parent or caretaker. This is a parental responsibility, but in some cases of child abuse and neglect or for other reasons, the state may have to assume responsibility for supervision. (See also CHILD IN NEED OF SUPERVISION)
2) Process in social work practice whereby workers review cases with supervisors to assure case progress, to sharpen the workers' knowledge and skill, and to assure maintenance of agency policies and procedures. Unlike many practitioners in law and medicine, social workers do not generally practice independently or make totally independent judgments. In general, social work supervisors hold Master's degrees, but in some local public agencies these supervisors may be just out of graduate school and have little experience. Since good supervision is a critical factor in reducing the problem of staff burnout and staff flight, it is important for child protective service agencies to provide training and continuing education opportunities for supervisors.

SUPPORTIVE SERVICES
Supportive services are a wide range of human services which provide assistance to families or individuals so that they are more nearly able to fulfill their potential for positive growth and behavior. The concept implies that individuals have basic strengths which need to be recognized, encouraged, and aided. Thus, a wide range of financial, educational, vocational, child care, counseling, recreational, and other services might be seen as supportive if they do indeed emphasize the strengths of people and de-emphasize their occasional needs for help in overcoming destructive and debilitating factors which may affect their lives.

SURROGATE PARENT
A person other than a biological parent who, living within or outside the target home, provides nurturance. This person may be self-selected or assigned to fulfill parental functions. A surrogate parent may nurture children or abusive or neglectful parents who were themselves abused as children and therefore are in need of a nurturing parental model. (See also PARENT AIDE)

SUSPECTED CHILD ABUSE AND NEGLECT
Reason to believe that child abuse or neglect has or is occurring in a given family. Anyone can in good faith report this to the local mandated agency, which will investigate and protect the child as necessary. However, all states have statutes which provide that members of certain professions must report and that failure to do so is punishable by fine or imprisonment. For specific criteria for suspecting child abuse or neglect, see INDICATORS OF CHILD ABUSE AND NEGLECT and FAMILIES-AT-RISK.

SUTURE
1) A type of immovable joint in which the connecting surfaces of the bones are closely united, as in the skull.
2) The stitches made by a physician that close a wound.

SYPHILIS (See VENEREAL DISEASE)

TARGET CHILD (See SPECIAL CHILD)

TEMPORAL
Referring to the side of the head.

TEMPORARY CUSTODY (See CUSTODY)

TEMPORARY PLACEMENT
Voluntary or involuntary short term removal of a child from his/her own home, primarily when a child's safety or well-being is threatened or endangered, or when a family crisis can be averted by such action. Temporary placement may be in a relative's home, receiving home or shelter, foster home, or institution. Temporary placement should be considered only if service to the child and family within the home, such as use of a homemaker or day care, is determined to be insufficient to protect or provide for the child or if it is unavailable. If the home situation does not improve while the child is in temporary placement, long term placement may be warranted. However, authorities agree that too many temporary placements unnecessarily become permanent placements. (See also CUSTODY)

TERMINATION OF PARENTAL RIGHTS (TPR)
A legal proceeding freeing a child from his/her parents' claims so that the child can be adopted by others without the parents' written consent. The legal bases for termination differ from state to state, but most statutes include abandonment as a ground for TPR. (See also ABANDONMENT)

TESTIMONY
A declaration or statement made to establish a fact, especially one made under oath in court.

THREATENED HARM
Substantial risk of harm to a child, including physical or mental injury, sexual assault, neglect of physical and/or educational needs, inadequate supervision, or abandonment.

TITLE IV (See SOCIAL SECURITY ACT)

TITLE V (See SOCIAL SECURITY ACT)

TITLE XIX (TITLE 19, MEDICAID) (See SOCIAL SECURITY ACT)

TITLE XX (See SOCIAL SECURITY ACT)

TORUS FRACTURE (See FRACTURE)

TRABECULA
A general term for a supporting or anchoring strand of tissue.

TRAUMA
An internal or external injury or wound brought about by an outside force. Usually trauma means injury by violence, but it may also apply to the wound caused by any surgical procedure. Trauma may be caused accidentally or, as in a ease of physical abuse, non-acciden-tally. Trauma is also a term applied to psychological discomfort or symptoms resulting from an emotional shock or painful experience.

TRAUMA X
Designation used by some hospitals for a child abuse and neglect program.

TREATMENT FOSTER CARE
Foster care for children with diagnosed emotional and/or behavioral problems in which foster parents with special training and experience become part of a treatment team working with a particular child. Treatment foster care may be indicated for abused or severely neglected children.

TREATMENT OF CHILD ABUSE AND NEGLECT
1) Helping parents or caretakers stop child abuse and neglect and assisting them and their children to function adequately as a family unit. 2) Providing temporary placement and services as necessary for abused or neglected children until their parents can assume their parental responsibilities without threat to the children's welfare. 3) Terminating parental rights and placing the children in an adoptive home if the parents abandon the children or absolutely cannot be helped. Experts believe that 80% to 85% of abusive and neglectful parents can be helped to function without threat to their children's welfare and, more often than not, without temporary placement of the children if sufficient supportive services are available.

Treatment for child abuse and neglect should include treatment for the abused and neglected children as well as for the parents.

Treatment for child abuse and neglect includes both crisis intervention and long term treatment. The mandated agency may provide services directly or by purchase of service from other agencies. Since a multiplicity of services is often necessary, a case management approach to treatment is usually most effective (see CASE MANAGEMENT). Because mandated agencies necessarily focus on investigation of suspected cases and crisis intervention, long term treatment is best assured through use of a community team (see COMMUNITY TEAM).

Both crisis intervention and long term treatment will usually require a mix of supportive and therapeutic services. Supportive services could include homemakers, day care, foster grandparents, parent education, health care, family planning, recreational activities, housing assistance, transportation, legal services, employment training and placement, financial counseling and assistance. Therapeutic services could include psychotherapy, casework, lay therapy from parent aides, group therapy, family or couple therapy, and self-help such as Parents Anonymous.

TURGOR
Condition of being swollen and congested. This can refer to normal or other fullness.

TWENTY-FOUR HOUR EMERGENCY SERVICES
Local services available at all times to receive reports and make immediate investigations of suspected cases of child abuse and severe neglect and to perform crisis intervention if necessary. The mode of providing twenty-four hour emergency services varies in different localities. However, often mandated agency protective service workers are on call for specific evening and weekend assignments. Often the after-hours number rings the police or sheriffs department which then contacts the assigned worker. (See also COMPREHENSIVE EMERGENCY SERVICES)

UNFOUNDED REPORT
Any report of suspected child abuse or neglect made to the mandated agency for which it is determined that there is no probable cause to believe that abuse or neglect has occurred. Mandated agencies may or may not remove unfounded reports from their records after a period of time. (See also EXPUNGEMENT)

VASCULAR
Of the blood vessels.

VENEREAL DISEASE
Any disease transmitted by sexual contact. The two most common forms of venereal disease are gonorrhea and syphilis. Presence of a venereal disease in a child may indicate that the mother was infected with the disease during the pregnancy, or it may be evidence of sexual abuse.

VERBAL ABUSE (See CHILD ABUSE AND NEGLECT)

VERIFICATION OF CHILD ABUSE AND NEGLECT
Substantiation of child abuse or neglect following investigation of suspected cases by mandated agency workers and/or assessment by a diagnostic team. Also referred to as a founded report.

VICTIM-PRECIPITATED ABUSE (See SPECIAL CHILD)

VISITING FRIEND (See PARENT AIDE)

VITAL SIGNS
Signs manifesting life, such as respiratory rate, heartbeat, pulse, blood pressure, and eye responses.

VOIR DIRE
1. Procedure during which lawyers question prospective jurors to determine their biases, if any.
2. Procedure in which lawyers question expert witnesses regarding their qualifications before the experts are permitted to give opinion testimony.

VOLUNTARY PLACEMENT
Act of a parent in which custody of his/her child is relinquished without a formal court proceeding. Sometimes called voluntary relinquishment.

VOLUNTEER ROLES
1) Extension and enrichment of direct services to families by unpaid, screened, trained, and supervised persons who generally lack professional training. Common roles are parent aides, child care workers, outreach workers, or staff for helplines. 2) Development and advocacy of child abuse and neglect programs by unpaid persons through participation on community councils, agency boards, or community committees. Scarce resources in relation to the magnitude of the problem of child abuse and neglect demands that volunteers be used increasingly.

WANTON
Extremely reckless or malicious. Often used in court proceedings in conjunction with "willful" to establish certain kinds of unlawful behavior only vaguely distinguished from careless but lawful conduct.

WARRANT
Document issued by a judge, authorizing the arrest or detention of a person or the search of a place and seizure of specified items in that place. Although a judge need not hold a hearing before issuing a warrant and although the party to be arrested or whose property will be seized need not be notified, the judge must still be given "reasonable cause to believe" that a crime has occurred and that the warrant is necessary in the apprehension and conviction of the criminal.

WHIPLASH-SHAKEN INFANT SYNDROME
Injury to an infant or child that results from that child having been shaken, usually as a misguided means of discipline. The most common symptoms, which can be inflicted by seemingly harmless shakings, are bleeding and/or detached retinas and other bleeding inside the head. Repeated instances of shaking and resultant injuries may eventually cause mental and developmental disabilities. (See also SUBDURAL HEMATOMA)

WILLFUL
Done with understanding of the act and the intention that the act and its natural consequences should occur. Some conduct

becomes unlawful or negligent only when it is done willfully.

WITNESS
1. A person who has seen or heard something.
2. A person who is called upon to testify in a court hearing.

WORKER BURNOUT (See Staff Burnout)

WORK-UP
Study of a patient, often in a hospital, in order to provide information for diagnosis. A full work-up includes past medical and family histories, present condition and symptoms, laboratory, and, possibly, X-ray studies.

WORLD OF ABNORMAL REARING (WAR)
A generational cycle of development in which abused or neglected children tend to grow up to be abusive or neglectful parents unless intervention occurs to break the cycle. The diagram which follows outlines the WAR cycle. (Heifer)

X-RAYS
Photographs made by means of X-rays. X-rays are one of the most important tools available to physicians in the diagnosis of physical child abuse or battering. With X-rays, or radiologic examinations, physicians can observe not only the current bone injuries of a child, but also any past injuries that may exist in various stages of healing. This historical information contributes significantly to the assessment of a suspected case of child abuse. Radiologic examination is also essential to distinguish organic diseases that may cause bone breakage from physical child abuse.

Acronyms

AAP	American Academy of Pediatrics	**PET**	Parent Effectiveness Training
ACSW	Academy of Certified Social Workers	**PINS**	Person in Need of Supervision
ACYF	Administration for Children, Youth and Families (formerly Office of Child Development), U.S. Department of Health, Education and Welfare	**CPS**	Child Protective Services
		CWLA	Child Welfare League of America
		DART	Detection, Admission, Reporting, and Treatment (multidisciplinary team)
		DD	Developmental Disability
ADC	Aid to Dependent Children (Title IV-A of the Social Security Act) (also referred to as AFDC)	**DHEW**	U.S. Department of Health, Education and Welfare (also referred to as HEW)
AF	Alleged Father	**DPW**	Department of Public Welfare
AFDC	Aid to Families with Dependent Children (Title IV-A of the Social Security Act) (also referred to as ADC)	**DSS**	Department of Social Services
		EPSDT	Early and Periodic Screening, Diagnosis, and Treatment
		ER	Emergency Room
AHA	American Humane Association	**FTT**	Failure to Thrive
AMA	Against Medical Advice; American Medical Association	**GAL**	*Guardian ad l item*
		HEW	U.S. Department of Health, Education and Welfare (also referred to as DHEW)
APA	American Psychiatric Association; American Psychological Association		
		IP	Identified Patient
APWA	American Public Welfare Association	**LD**	Learning Disability
		MINS	Minor in Need of Supervision
CALM	Child Abuse Listening Mediation	**NASW**	National Association of Social Workers
CAN	Child Abuse and Neglect		
CAP	Community Action Program	**NCCA**	National Center for Child Advocacy
CDAHA	Children's Division of the American Humane Association	**NCCAN**	National Center on Child Abuse and Neglect
CDF	Children's Defense Fund		
CES	Comprehensive Emergency Services	**NIH**	National Institutes of Health
		NIMH	National Institute of Mental Health
CHIPS	Child in Need of Protection and Supervision	**OCD**	Office of Child Development (now Adminstration for Children, Youth and Families). U.S. Department of Health, Education and Welfare
CLL	Childhood Level of Living Scale		
CNS	Central Nervous System		
	Office of Human Development Services), U.S. Department of Health, Education and Welfare	**OHD**	Office of Human Development (now
OHDS	Office of Human Development Services (formerly Office of Human Development), U.S. Department of Health, Education and Welfare	**PL 93-247**	Child Abuse Prevention and Treatment Act
		SCAN	Suspected Child Abuse and Neglect
PA	Parents Anonymous		

SIDS	Sudden Infant Death Syndrome	**VD**	Venereal Disease
STD	Sexually Transmissible Disease	**WAR**	World of Abnormal Rearing
TPR	Termination of Parental Rights	**WIN**	Work Incentive Program
UM	Unmarried Mother		

www.ingramcontent.com/pod-product-compliance
Lightning Source LLC
Chambersburg PA
CBHW080323020526
44117CB00035B/2622